JUDEO-SPANISH BALLADS
FROM BOSNIA

THE ELEVENTH PUBLICATION
IN THE HANEY FOUNDATION SERIES
UNIVERSITY OF PENNSYLVANIA

UNIVERSITY OF PENNSYLVANIA
PUBLICATIONS IN FOLKLORE AND FOLKLIFE

Editor: Kenneth S. Goldstein; *Associate Editors:* Dan Ben-Amos,
Tristram Potter Coffin, Dell Hymes, John Szwed, Don Yoder;
Consulting Editors: Samuel G. Armistead, Maria Brooks, Daniel
Hoffman, David Sapir, Biljana Šljivić-Šimšić

No. 1 HENRY GLASSIE
   *Pattern in the Material Folk Culture
   of the Eastern United States*

No. 2 ALAN BRODY
   *The English Mummers and Their Plays:
   Traces of Ancient Mystery*

No. 3 PIERRE MARANDA AND ELLI KÖNGÄS MARANDA, EDITORS
   Structural Analysis of Oral Tradition

No. 4 SAMUEL G. ARMISTEAD AND JOSEPH H. SILVERMAN, EDITORS
   WITH THE COLLABORATION
   OF BILJANA ŠLJIVIĆ-ŠIMŠIĆ
   Judeo-Spanish Ballads from Bosnia

Judeo-Spanish Ballads from Bosnia

Edited by

SAMUEL G. ARMISTEAD   JOSEPH H. SILVERMAN

with the collaboration of

BILJANA ŠLJIVIĆ-ŠIMŠIĆ

UNIVERSITY OF PENNSYLVANIA PRESS
PHILADELPHIA

1971

Publication of this book has been made possible by a grant from the
Haney Foundation of the University of Pennsylvania.
A grant from the University of California at Santa Cruz has also
aided the publication of this book.

ISBN: 0-8122-7631-0

Manufactured in Germany by J. J. Augustin, Glückstadt

TO THE MEMORY

OF

CYNTHIA M. CREWS

CONTENTS

ABBREVIATIONS

AEM = *Anuario de Estudios Medievales*, Barcelona
AFC = See Bibliography: Peninsular Ballads
ART = See Bibliography: Peninsular Ballads
ASW = See Bibliography: Peninsular Ballads
Avenç = See Bibliography: Peninsular Ballads
BAE = *Boletín de la Real Academia Española*, Madrid
BAH = *Boletín de la Real Academia de la Historia*, Madrid
BHi = *Bulletin Hispanique*, Bordeaux
BHS = *Bulletin of Hispanic Studies*, Liverpool
CE = *Cultura Española*, Madrid
CPE = See Bibliography: Peninsular Ballads
DgF = See Bibliography: European Ballads
DRH = See Bibliography: Judeo-Spanish Ballads
DVM = See Bibliography: European Ballads
HR = *Hispanic Review*, Philadelphia
JFI = *Journal of the Folklore Institute*, Bloomington
MAe = *Medium Aevum*, Oxford
MLN = *Modern Language Notes*, Baltimore
MP = See Bibliography: Judeo-Spanish Ballads
MPh = *Modern Philology*, Chicago
NRFH = *Nueva Revista de Filología Hispánica*, Mexico City
NSR = See Bibliography: Judeo-Spanish Ballads
OCPC = See Bibliography: Peninsular Ballads
Primavera = See Bibliography: Peninsular Ballads
REJ = *Revue des Études Juives*, Paris
RFE = *Revista de Filología Española*, Madrid
RFH = *Revista de Filología Hispánica*, Buenos Aires
RHi = *Revue Hispanique*, Paris
RIHGB = *Revista do Instituto Histórico e Geográfico Brasileiro*, Rio
de Janeiro
RL = *Revista Lusitana*, Lisbon
RLC = *Revue de Littérature Comparée*, Paris
RLiR = *Revue de Linguistique Romane*, Paris
RPC = See Bibliography: Peninsular Ballads
RPh = *Romance Philology*, Berkeley
RPM = See Bibliography: Peninsular Ballads
RTCN = See Bibliography: Peninsular Ballads
Sef = *Sefarad*, Madrid

SICh = See Bibliography: Judeo-Spanish Ballads
Spomenica = See Bibliography: Judeo-Spanish Ballads
WF = *Western Folklore*, Berkeley
Vasconcellos, "Bibl. do Povo" = See Bibliography: Peninsular Ballads
VRP = See Bibliography: Peninsular Ballads
Yoná = See Bibliography: Judeo-Spanish Ballads
ZRPh = *Zeitschrift für Romanische Philologie*, Tübingen

INTRODUCTION

For the Sephardic Jews, exiled from Spain in 1492, the western areas of the Ottoman Empire held forth the promise of a place of refuge not unlike their Hispanic homeland. At the end of the Middle Ages, both the Iberian and the Balkan Peninsulas were the home of orientalized European societies, whose culture, language, and folk literature reflected the intimate symbiosis of believers in the three religions—Christians, Jews, and Moslems. Populous communities of Hispano-Jewish exiles were established at Salonika and Istanbul shortly after the expulsion. Sephardic Jews seem, however, not to have reached Bosnia directly from Spain, but rather through subsequent emigration from other Ottoman communities, principally Salonika. By the middle of the sixteenth century, the Sephardim were firmly established at Sarajevo, the chief city of Bosnia, which to the present day has included a Spanish-speaking Jewish community among its multilingual and multireligious population.[1]

Diverted from the mainstream of Hispanic culture at the end of the Middle Ages, Judeo-Spanish language and folk literature—despite the absorption of numerous Balkan elements—constitute in essence a living, contemporary document of late fifteenth-century Spanish linguistic and folkloric forms and, as such, are of inestimable value to Hispanists and folklorists alike. Judeo-Spanish culture in Bosnia today is, however, rapidly approaching extinction. With the Europeanization of the Balkans in the early decades of the twentieth century, the Spanish Jews of Sarajevo began to substitute Serbo-Croatian—with German and French as second languages—for the Judeo-Spanish

---

1. On the history of the Sarajevo community see M. Levy, *Die Sephardim in Bosnien: Ein Beitrag zur Geschichte der Juden auf der Balkanhalbinsel* (Sarajevo, 1911) and id., *Sefardi u Bosni: Prilog istoriji Jevreja na Balkanskom poluostrvu* (Belgrade, 1969). See also K. Baruch, "El judeo-español de Bosnia," *RFE*, XVII (1930), 113–151: p. 117; M. Alvar, "Sefardíes en una novela de Ivo Andrić," *RLiR*, XXXI (1967), 267–271, and E. Giménez Caballero's impressionistic but revealing "Judíos españoles de Sarajevo," *Judaica* (Buenos Aires), Año VII, Nos. 73–75 (July–Sept. 1939), pp. 37–39. Numerous aspects of Bosnian Sephardic history are taken up in the publication *Spomenica: 400 godina od dolaska Jevreja u Bosnu i Hercegovinu (1566–1966)*. See also the important review article by J. O. Prenz, "Vicisitudes del judeo-español de Bosnia," *Romanica* (La Plata, Argentina), I (1968), 163–173. The tragedy of 1939–1945 reduced Sarajevo's Jewish community from 12,000 to 1000 souls (Alvar, *op. cit.*, p. 270, *n.* 1).

For the historical background of the expulsion of the Jews from Spain see J. Amador de los Ríos, *Historia social, política y religiosa de los judíos de España y Portugal* (Madrid, 1960), esp. pp. 725–758; Y. Baer, *A History of the Jews in Christian Spain*, 2 vols. (Philadelphia, 1961), esp. II, 424–443.

dialect, which for almost four centuries had served as the language both of domestic intimacy and of Jewish community affairs. Today, Serbo-Croation is the native speech of most Sephardim in Bosnia, while Judeo-Spanish has been relegated to the status of a nostalgically revered echo of a way of life which has ceased to exist forever.

The traditional balladry of the Bosnian Sephardim has until recently remained largely unknown to most Western scholars. However, ballad-collecting among the Bosnian Jews was not neglected, as the texts reedited here bear witness.² Still, the two major published collections of Bosnian Judeo-Spanish *romances* first saw print in such singularly inaccessible form that they have remained virtually unavailable to Western Hispanists and students of folk literature. Kalmi Baruch's "Španske romanse bosanskih Jevreja," including eighteen ballad texts, was printed in 1933 in a yearbook sponsored by two Jewish beneficent societies of Sarajevo and Belgrade. Until Moshe Attias called attention to it in his *Romancero sefaradí* (1st ed., Jerusalem, 1956), Baruch's important collection had gone altogether unnoticed in Western ballad publications. Even now, no copy seems to be available anywhere in the United States. References in Paul Bénichou's *Romancero judeo-español de Marruecos* (Madrid, 1968), in Manuel Alvar's *Poesía tradicional de los judíos españoles* (Mexico City, 1966), and in our own writings as well have had to depend upon photographic reproductions of the same, possibly unique copy housed at the Jewish National and University Library in Jerusalem. Even more ephemeral and recondite is the bibliographical status of a series of twenty-one magnificent texts printed in 1939–1940 in the newspaper *Jevrejski Glas* ("The Jewish Voice") of Sarajevo. They survive in the form of mostly undated clippings in the possession of the Rev. Dr. Solomon Gaon of London, who was generous enough to place them at our disposal.³

2. For a brief survey of ballad collecting in the various Eastern communities see our "Judeo-Spanish Ballads in a MS by Salomon Israel Cherezli," *Studies in Honor of M. J. Benardete* (New York, 1965), pp. 367–387 (abbr. SICh). See also *Diez romances hispánicos en un manuscrito sefardí de la Isla de Rodas* (Pisa, 1962), pp. 11–13 (abbr. DRH). On recent collecting in Morocco see P. Bénichou, "Nouvelles explorations du romancero judéo-espagnol marocain," *BHi*, LXIII (1961), 217–248 (now revised as "Exploraciones del Romancero judeo-español marroquí entre 1951 y 1966" in *Romancero judeo-español de Marruecos*, pp. 305–359). Add to this I. J. Katz's brief report on our 1962 Moroccan field trip in *Bulletin of the International Folk Music Council* (London), XXIII (April, 1963), 15.

See the bibliography at the end of the present publication for works referred to by abbreviations or short titles.

3. See the reference to these clippings in the *Catálogo de la Exposición Bibliográfica Sefardí Mundial* (Madrid, 1959), No. 749.

A word must be said concerning other published and unedited sources of Bosnian Judeo-Spanish ballads. As early as 1903 Leo Wiener collected and edited, in his "Songs of the Spanish Jews in the Balkan Peninsula,"[4] several *romances* recited by a Bosnian informant in Belgrade. Wiener's ballads include *La fuerza de la sangre* + *El caballero burlado* (No. 7), *La vuelta del marido* (*i*; 8), *La malcasada del pastor* (9), *Landarico* (11), and *El encuentro del padre* (12). Ángel Pulido Fernández' *Intereses nacionales: Españoles sin patria y la raza sefardí* (Madrid, 1905), includes two Bosnian ballads: *Virgilios* (pp. 296f.), from a Berlin informant of Eastern origin, which agrees very closely with other Bosnian texts, and *Escogiendo novia* (p. 79), the only known Eastern Sephardic version, which was sent to Pulido by a Sarajevan resident of Trieste. Manuel Manrique de Lara, probably the greatest Judeo-Spanish ballad collector of all time, included Sarajevo in his 1911 Balkan itinerary. Samples of his magnificent, largely unedited collection, now in the Menéndez Pidal archive, have over the years gradually been printed. Published Bosnian texts collected by M. de Lara include *La dama y el pastor*,[5] *El idólatra*,[6] *La fuerza de la sangre*, *La canción del huérfano*,[7] and *La vuelta del hijo maldecido*.[8] Mrs. Cynthia Crews, peerless explorer of the spoken language and early *Sprachdenkmäler* of the Balkan Sephardim, also collected *romances* in Sarajevo. Seven excellent versions (*Hero y Leandro, Malcasada del pastor, Conde Olinos, Reina y cautiva, Melisenda insomne* + *Choza del deses-*

4. *MPh*, I (1903–1904), 205–216, 259–274.

5. A synthetic text, including readings from Sarajevo, appears in R. Menéndez Pidal, *Romancero hispánico*, 2 vols. (Madrid, 1953), I, 341–342.

6. D. Catalán, "La recolección romancística en Canarias," in M. Morales and M. J. López de Vergara, *Romancerillo canario* (La Laguna, 1955), pp. 28 and 30. See now *Por campos del Romancero* (Madrid, 1970), pp. 270–271.

7. Synthetic texts of *Fuerza* and *Canción*, taking into account readings of versions collected by Manrique de Lara in Sarajevo, appear in D. Catalán, "A caza de romances raros en la tradición portuguesa," *Actas do III Colóquio Internacional de Estudos Luso-Brasileiros*, I (Lisbon, 1959), 445–477. A revised version of this study now forms part of *Por campos del Romancero*. See esp. pp. 234–235 and 243–245.

8. *Romancero tradicional de las lenguas hispánicas (Español-portugués-catalán-sefardí)*, III, ed. D. Catalán (Madrid, 1969), Section III, Nos. 14–20 and 23.

Is Manrique de Lara's Belgrade version of *La muerte de Alejandro* (= MP 44) of Bosnian origin? See "Romances españoles en los Balkanes," *Blanco y Negro* (Madrid), Año 26 (Jan. 2, 1916), No. 1285 (text II). On the text's geographic attribution see V. T. Mendoza, *El romance español y el corrido mejicano* (Mexico City, 1939), p. 36. For two other musical texts from Belgrade see *Romancero hispánico*, I, 401 (= *Landarico* and *Conde Olinos*). On versions of *Celinos y la adúltera* collected by M. de Lara in Sarajevo see our *Judeo-Spanish Ballad Chapbooks of Y. A. Yoná*, No. 17. Unedited Bosnian versions of *La cabalgada de Peranzules*, *La gentil porquera*, and *La mujer de Juan Lorenzo* are mentioned in *Romancero Hispánico*, I, 316; II, 315, 335.

perado, *Mujer engañada*, and *Adúltera* [*á-a*]), collected in November
1929, were generously forwarded to us by Mrs. Crews and will be
edited in our projected volumes of ballads recorded from oral tradition.
In his linguistic treatise "El judeo-español de Bosnia," Kalmi Baruch
quotes a single verse of what must be an otherwise unknown Bosnian
version of *Tiempo es el caballero*, an extremely rare *romance*, of which
the two initial verses have been reported from Vienna—possibly of
Bosnian origin—and the Island of Rhodes.[9] A putative source of
Bosnian Sephardic *romances* is Isaac Levy's *Chants judéo-espagnols*
(London, [1959]), but regrettably the texts are not geographically identified. By comparing Levy's versions with other published texts we may
tentatively assign his *Vuelta del marido* (*i*; No. 7), *Melisenda insomne* +
Choza del desesperado (12), *Landarico* (14), *Celinos* + *Vos labraré un
pendón* (67), and *Adúltera* (*á-a*; 85) to the Bosnian tradition.[10] In
1966 five Bosnian Sephardic ballads were printed in the memorial
publication *Spomenica: 400 godina od dolaska Jevreja u Bosnu i Hercegovinu*. Four of these texts reproduce Kalmi Baruch's *Vuelta del
marido* (*i*), *Vuelta del hijo maldecido*, *Landarico*, and *Encuentro del
padre*. The fifth, a fine version of the extremely rare *¿Por qué no
cantáis la bella?*, carries no identification and is apparently printed
here for the first time. Since copies of *Spomenica* are not easily found in
the United States, we reproduce this version below:

> Estávase la condesa   asentada en su portal.
> Agujica de oro en mano,   filando está la perla.
>   ¡Hay, galana y bella!
> Por ahí passó un caballero,   criado del rey su padre:
> —¿De qué no cantáis, galana,   de qué no cantáis, la bella?
>   ¡Hay, galana y bella!
> 5 —Ni canto, ni cantaría,   que'l mi amor no está en la tienda.
> Preso lo tiene aquel rey,   aquel rey de Inglaterra.
>   ¡Hay, galana y bella!
> Escribir quiero una carta   de mano y de mi letra;
> mandársela a aquel rey,   aquel rey de Inglaterra.
>   ¡Hay, galana y bella!

---

9. The verse, "paríldu, infánta, parildu / ke ansí me parió mi madre a mí"
(Baruch, "El judeo-español," p. 139), corresponds to *Primavera* 158, v. 7:
"Parildo, dijo, señora, / que así hizo mi madre a mí." Menéndez Pidal records the
two Viennese verses (MP 103); on the Rhodian fragment—a not inappropriate
contamination in a version of *Una ramica de ruda*—see DRH, pp. 52–53, *nn*.
45–46. The first verse of the ballad also contaminates Attias' Salonikan text of
Bodas en París (No. 32, vv. 54–55).
10. See our review in *NRFH*, XIV (1960), 345–349.

Que me solte al mi marido   de prisiones y cadenas.
10 Y si no me lo soltara,   armar quiero una gran guerra.
      ¡Hay, galana y bella!
Galeones por las mares,   gente y armas por la tierra.
Y por falta de capetanes,   yo iré a la delantera.
      ¡Hay, galana y bella!
Para que digan la gente: "¡Viva, viva tal guerrera!
14 Que por amor de su marido   llevó ansí una gran guerra."
      ¡Hay, galana y bella![11]

The most striking feature of the Bosnian Sephardic tradition, considered in its entirety, is its almost completely novelesque character. In this regard, Bosnian balladry seems strangely modern, almost as if it were a regional variant of the Peninsular *Romancero*; although, of course, many of the Bosnian Sephardim's individual *romances novelescos* are notably rare and archaic in character (for example, *Idólatra, Canción del huérfano, ¿Por qué no cantáis?, Don Bueso y su hermana, Parto en lejas tierras, Raptor pordiosero*). The Bosnian tradition has preserved some remarkable legendary themes, as in *La fuerza de la sangre* (the infant hero's exposure, obscure upbringing, and noble bloodlines), *El encuentro del padre* (the hero's quest for his father), and the thaumaturgical music of *El chuflete*. Yet it is surprising to note the absence of some of the *Romancero*'s most thematically archaic categories; ballads deriving from Spanish epicry, Carolingian *romances* (a gravely eroded *Melisenda insomne* being the lone exception), and themes concerned with Spanish history all seem to be completely lacking.[12] Notable too is the absence of ballads on Biblical matter. Bosnia was, in effect, a lateral area with respect to the great Sephardic metropolis of Salonika. Yet this is a curious case in which an outlying fringe region is less conservative than the cultural center, for Salonika,

11. *Spomenica*, p. 323, from an unsigned section entitled "Iz folklora bosanskih sefarada," pp. 321–326. Concerning the ballad ¿*Por qué no cantáis la bella?*, see R. Menéndez Pidal's note to A. Morel-Fatio, "Un romance à retrouver," *RFE*, II (1915), 371–373, where Sarajevan versions collected by M. de Lara are used, together with variants from Tangier, Salonika, and Larissa to construct a synthetic text. See also P. Bénichou's fundamental study "La belle qui ne saurait chanter: Notes sur un motif de poésie populaire," *RLC*, XXVIII (1954), 257–281; a supplementary article by M. I. Henderson and J. B. Trend, "Brântome's Spanish Ballad: A MS. from Winchester," *BHS*, XXXII (1955), 63–72; and also Menéndez Pidal, *Romancero hispánico*, I, 328; II, 218, 338, 350, 409, *n*. 6; Bénichou, *Romancero*, pp. 169–174.
We are grateful to Professor Andreas Tietze for generously making available to us his copy of *Spomenica*.
12. See K. Baruch's commentary below (Section B, part III).

of all the Eastern communities, has best preserved the ancient epic, Carolingian, and historical themes of Spain's medieval *Romancero*.[13]

In the present publication we have sought to remedy the bibliographical inaccessibility of Bosnian Sephardic balladry by editing three fundamentally important sources: Kalmi Baruch's "Španski romanse" (with the musical transcriptions of B. Jungić), the *Jevrejski Glas* ballads, and a brief, previously unknown eighteenth-century MS collection. We have identified and annotated Kalmi Baruch's texts and, with the valued collaboration of Professor Biljana Šljivić-Šimšić of the University of Pennsylvania, his Serbo-Croatian commentary has been translated into English. The *romances* published in *Jevrejski Glas* have likewise been classified and edited. To these two twentieth-century collections we have added five precious, previously unedited eighteenth-century Bosnian ballads from MS Heb. 8⁰ 2946 of the Jewish National and University Library.

The present publication is purely documentary in character. No attempt has been made to study in depth the ballads edited here. We reserve such a task for the commentary to our projected multivolume edition of Sephardic *romances* collected from oral tradition, to which the present volume constitutes a necessary bibliographical preliminary.[14] Here we have merely provided—in the hope that they may be of use to non–Hispanist folklorists—English abstracts of each ballad text-type. In most cases, we have limited our notes to the identification of contaminations and verse borrowings; for the bibliography of Judeo-Spanish variants and of analogs in the Hispanic and European traditions we have consistently referenced only a small number of indispensable publications containing extensive bibliographical ap-

---

13. See our article "Dos romances fronterizos" and Nos. 1–9 of our edition of Y. A. Yoná's ballads. The present appraisal of the Bosnian Sephardic ballad tradition was written largely on the basis of published materials and before we had had the opportunity, at the generous invitation of Diego Catalán, to work during the summer of 1970 with the magnificent unedited ballad collection in Menéndez Pidal's archives. Our *Índice de romances judeo-españoles inéditos en la colección de R. Menéndez Pidal* (now being prepared in collaboration with D. Catalán) will significantly augment the number of text-types known from the Bosnian *Romancero*, though it will probably not alter our appraisal of the basically novelesque character of that tradition.

When the present work was already in proofs, Diego Catalán was kind enough to call our attention to his study of *El bonetero de la trapería* ("Una jacarilla barroca hoy tradicional en Extremadura y en Oriente," *Revista de Estudios Extremeños*, VIII [1952], 377–387), now thoroughly revised and amplified in *Por campos del Romancero*, pp. 283–301. See pp. 283–284 for the Bosnian version.

14. Cf. the detailed studies accompanying our edition of *The Judeo-Spanish Ballad Chapbooks of Y. A. Yoná*.

paratus (Attias, Bénichou, DRH, NSR, Yoná). Only when a given text-type is absent from all these works or where Hispanic or European parallels may have previously gone unnoticed, do we provide more extensive bibliographical coverage. Motifs listed in S. Thompson's *Index*, which appear in the ballads edited here, have been incorporated into our "English Abstracts" and are also brought together in a special index at the back of the book.

In closing, we wish to thank the following friends and colleagues for their valued help and advice: Moshe Attias (Jerusalem), Meir Benayahu (Jerusalem), the late Cynthia M. Crews (Leeds), Kenneth S. Goldstein (Pennsylvania), Wayland D. Hand (U.C.L.A.), Iacob M. Hassán (Madrid), Israel J. Katz (Columbia), and Andreas Tietze (U.C.L.A.). To Dr. I. Joel, Deputy Director of the Jewish National and University Library, we express our sincere gratitude for his kindness in granting us permission to publish the *romances* in MS 8⁰ 2946. To the Rev. Dr. Solomon Gaon go our heartfelt thanks for his generosity in offering us the *Jevrejski Glas* ballads. Miss Martha Lowenstine's expert and patient editorial help has contributed significantly to the readability of our text. Finally, we wish to thank The Haney Foundation (University of Pennsylvania) and the University of California (Santa Cruz) for generous financial support which has made possible the publication of this book.

A.

FIVE EIGHTEENTH-CENTURY BOSNIAN BALLADS

(Jewish National and University Library, MS Heb. 8⁰ 2946)

T extual evidence of Judeo-Spanish traditional balladry prior to the final decades of the nineteenth century is notably sparse. From the first exiguous publications in Western journals in the 1880s and 1890s[1] and the earliest known Ladino ballad chapbook printed in Salonika by Y. A. Yoná (1891),[2] we must, going backward in time, bridge a one-hundred-year lacuna before reaching the seven precious Rhodian ballads in the manuscript of Yakov Hazán, copied in the final years of the eighteenth century,[3] and the song book of David Behar Moshé Ha-Cohen dated on the first of Adar II, 5554 (= 1794).[4] Almost

1. In 1885, H. Bidjarano included a fragment of *Virgilios* from Bucharest in his article "Los judíos españoles de Oriente: Lengua y literatura popular," *Boletín de la Institución Libre de Enseñanza* (Madrid), IX (1885), 23–27: p. 24a. Five years later, A. Sánchez Moguel edited a Turkish version of *La muerte del duque de Gandía* in "Un romance español en el dialecto de los judíos de Oriente," *BRAH*, XVI (1890), 497–509. J. Passy and J. Benaroya's "Spaniolisches Volkslied (Aus Ostrumelien)," *Der Urquell* (Leiden-Hamburg), New Series, I (1897), 206, a text of *Una ramica de ruda*, was the first ballad to be published with music (see Katz, *Judeo-Spanish Traditional Ballads from Jerusalem*, pp. 45, 181, *nn.* 35–36). Abraham Danon's "Recueil de romances judéo-espagnoles chantées en Turquie," published in 1896 (see bibliography), was the first major collection of Sephardic ballads.

In *De la poesía heroico-popular castellana* (Barcelona, 1874) M. Milá y Fontanals alludes to a Moroccan version of *Gerineldo + Conde Sol* (see the ed. by M. de Riquer and J. Molas [Barcelona, 1959], pp. 445–446, *n.* 2). The MS collection of the Grand Rabbi of Salonika Isaac Bohor Amaradji, now in the Menéndez Pidal archives, dates from 1860. See D. Catalán, "La recolección romancística en Canarias," in Morales and López de Vergara, *Romancerillo canario*, pp. 28, 30–31.

2. Yoná's *Sēfer gĕdúlaθ Mōšeh* (Salonika, 5651 [= 1891]) includes a version of *El paso del Mar Rojo*. See our "Algo más para la bibliografía de Y. A. Yoná," pp. 317–318, 324 (No. 12), and *Judeo-Spanish Ballad Chapbooks*, No. 9.

3. See our *Diez romances hispánicos*, p. 19.

4. Concerning this largely unedited collection see M. Attias, *Romancero sefaradí*, pp. 17, *n.* 44, and 330; for a ballad (*El idólatra*) from this MS see p. 157.

Also of probable eighteenth-century vintage is the Sabbatean MS, which contains versions of *Delgadina* and *Tarquino y Lucrecia*, described by M. Attias in "Ha-rômansah *Tarkînôs wĕ-Lûkreçîah* bi-kĕθāb-yād šabĕθa'î," *Šēbet wā-ʿĀm*, III (1959), 97–101. On the problem of the MS's date (the end of the first half of the eighteenth century) see M. Attias and G. Scholem, *Sēfer Šîrôθ wĕ-θišbāḥôθ šel ha-Šabĕθa'îm* (Tel Aviv, 1947), p. 18.

On the existence of other unedited eighteenth-century materials note Menéndez Pidal's allusion to versions of ¿ *Por qué no cantáis la bella*? "sacadas de dos manuscritos de Sarajevo en caracteres rabínicos de la segunda mitad del siglo XVIII" (*RFE*, II [1915], 373). A similar MS is mentioned by D. Catalán, "A caza de romances raros," p. 451, *n.* 8.

another century separates the Hazán and Cohen collections from three Balkan Sephardic ballads (*Virgilios, Reina y cautiva, Paso del Mar Rojo*) interpolated shortly after 1702 into the handwritten miscellany of Moses Ben-Michael Ha-Cohen, *Nĕʿîm Zĕmîrôθ* (MS British Museum Add. 26967).[5] Before this point we find two full centuries of mystery, illuminated only by the numerous *incipits* absorbed as tune indicators in various sixteenth- and seventeenth-century collections of *piyyutim*,[6] Thomas Coenen's 1667 Dutch translation of Sabbatai Zevi's *Melisenda* ballad,[7] and two Hispano-Portuguese *romances* (*El sacrificio de Isaac* and *La infantina*), destined to flourish in the North African Jewish tradition, edited from a seventeenth-century "miscelânea judaica" by José Leite de Vasconcellos.[8]

MS Heb. 8⁰ 2946 of the Jewish National and University Library (Jerusalem) offers the rare possibility of adding substantially to the early textual evidence of Eastern Judeo-Spanish balladry. This precious MS is briefly described in the *Catálogo de la Exposición Bibliográfica Sefardí Mundial* (Madrid, 1959): "Cantos populares. Manuscrito en ladino, turco y griego de Bosnia.—Siglo XVIII—Letra cursiva" (392). The linguistically variegated contents of MS 8⁰ 2946 include the five ballads we have edited here. While *Virgilios* (1) and *Rico Franco* (2) differ surprisingly little from versions current in modern oral tradition, the text of *Silvana* (3) shows several peculiarities which, to judge by similar phenomena present in González Llubera's version of *Las hermanas reina y cautiva* (after 1702), seem to be characteristic of earlier stages of Eastern Judeo-Spanish balladry. It was evidently written down at a time when Christian elements inherited from the *romances'* Peninsular origins were undergoing a process of erosion, which led in some cases to their elimination in the modern tradition.[9] *La infanta deshonrada* (4) offers the most satisfactory Eastern Sephardic text published to date, although a number of its assonances are spoiled (vv. 3–5) and it is notably abbreviated in comparison with the North

---

5. The ballads were published by Ig. González-Llubera, "Three Jewish Spanish Ballads...," *MAe*, VII (1938), 15–28.

6. See H. Avenary, "Études sur le cancionero judéo-espagnol (XVIe et XVIIe siècles)," *Sef*, XX (1960), 377–394; M. Frenk Alatorre, "El antiguo cancionero sefardí," *NRFH*, XIV (1960), 312–318. On *incipit* evidence from Morocco (early eighteenth century), see our forthcoming study on the Aben Çur *piyyutim*.

7. See R. Menéndez Pidal, "Un viejo romance cantado por Sabbatai Ceví," *Mediaeval Studies in Honor of J. D. M. Ford* (Cambridge, Mass., 1948), pp. 183–190.

8. "Dois romances peninsulares," *RFE*, IX (1922), 395–398.

9. See our "Christian Elements and De-Christianization," pp. 29–30 (section 4), 31.

African versions. This unique Bosnian version lacks the various contaminations (*Conde Alarcos*; the impregnating fountain; cf. *El mal encanto*), which encumber the three other published texts from Turkey and Salonika (Attias 23; Danon 10; Hemsi 19). Our Bosnian variant clearly preserves the nuptial dénouement of *Primavera* 160, which is either blurred or replaced by bloody vengeance in the modern texts. The version of *El encuentro del padre* (5) in MS 8° 2946 diverges radically from the modern variants and attests to a certain formulaic improvisation which has interesting parallels elsewhere in the *Romancero*.[10]

With two exceptions (*s* = *sin*; *ṣ* = *samekh*), our transliteration system follows that used in "Algo más para la bibliografía de Y. A. Yoná" (pp. 316–317) and in our edition of Yoná's chapbooks: ' = *aleph*; *b* = *beth*; *d* = *daleth*; *f* = *pe* with diacritic; *g* = *gimel*; *ǧ* = *gimel* with diacritic; *ḥ* = *ḥeth*; *k* = *qoph*; *l* = *lamedh*; *m* = *mem*; *n* = *nun*; *p* = *pe*; *r* = *reš*; *s* = *sin*; *ṣ* = *samekh*; *š* = *šin*; *t* = *teth*; *v* = *beth* with diacritic; *y* = *yodh*; *z* = *zayin*; *ž* = *zayin* with diacritic; *a* = *aleph* (except in graphic word-final position, where *a* = *he*); *e* and *i* = *yodh*; *o* and *u* = *waw*. When *a* appears alone as a separate word, it represents an *aleph* joined to the following word in the original. A curved line under *da* and *ra* indicates that these letters are written as digraphs in the MS. Letters supplied because of *scriptio defectiva* or abbreviation in the MS are italicized. Material filling scribal lapses and physical lacunae is placed in brackets. Punctuation and word division (except *a* and *de* + the definite articles) have been adjusted to modern norms.[11]

10. The ballad's ending is weak, in irregular assonance, and seems to have been put together using formulas and topoi borrowed from other songs. See "Alto, alto como el pino, / derecho como la flecha" (*Vuelta del marido* [mixed assonance]: Molho, *Literatura*, p. 82; Attias 19); the motif of the red beard appears in the same ballad ("una barvica roya tiene, / empesando a espuntar") and also recalls *Gaiferos jugador*: "Él [i.e., God] te dyyo barvika roša..." (Yoná, No. 5, v. 8); abandonment in a well may echo the Salonikan ballad of *Los siete hermanos y el pozo airón* (Attias 83). Compare our commentary to *Gaiferos jugador* (Yoná 5), a ballad whose original components have been almost completely replaced by formulas and motifs drawn from other, often quite unrelated sources. On the possibility of formulistic composition in Hispanic balladry see Bénichou's important comments to *La lavandera de San Juan* (*Romancero judeo-español*, pp. 357–359).

11. In the MS, the ending of the ballads is indicated by the Hebrew word θōm 'end', which is written three times following the final verse of each text.

1. *Virgilios* (MP 46)

Tra'isyyones al Don Virğile   'en los palaṣyyos del rey,
por amar 'una donzelyy'a   ke se yamava Zadé,
ni más alta, ni máṣ baša,   sovrina 'era del rey.
'I 'el rey 'esto ke lo ṣupyera,   'en kársel lo ḥu'e a meter
5 'i laṣ yaves dela kársel   kon sí selaṣ yeva 'él.
Paṣa tyenpo 'i vyene tyenpo   'i ninguno se akodra dél.
'I 'un díy'a ke 'el rey se va ala misa,   vido paṣar 'una mužer,
veṣtida 'entera de lutyyo   de kavesa asta los pyes.
Demandó 'el rey ala ṣu ğente   de kén 'era 'esta mužer,
10 veṣtida 'entera de lutyyo   de kavesa asta los pyes.
—Madre 'es del Don Virğile,   'el ke 'en prezo lo tyene.
—¡Akí, akí, mis kavalyeros,   loṣ ke de 'el mi pan koméš!
Digamoṣ preṣto la misa   'i vayygámolda a ver.
Ṣaltó la reyna 'i dišo: —Yo no la diré sin ver.
15 ¡Akí, akí, mis kavalyeros,   los ke de 'el mi pan koméš!
Ya se parten, ya ṣe 'iyan,   al Don Virğil ḥu'eron a ver.
—¿ Ké azéš, 'el Don Virğile?   —Byen ke tenga, Ṣenyyor rey.
Peynando los miṣ kaveyos,   kon la mi barva tambyén.
De ke 'entrí 'en 'estaṣ prizyoneṣ,   me 'enpeṣaron a kreṣer.
20 Agora, por miṣ pekadoṣ,   me ṣe 'enpeṣaron a 'enblankeṣer.
— ¿ Ké anyyoṣ, 'el Don Virğile,   ke 'en estaṣ prizyones 'estáš?
—Ṣyete anyyoṣ, 'el mi Ṣenyyor rey,   tres me mankan para dyes.
Ṣi le plaze al mi Ṣenyyor rey,   kumpliré los dyes 'i seš.
— ¡Akí, akí, mis kavalyeros,   loṣ ke de 'el mi pan koméš!
25 Tomaréš al Don Virğile,   al banyyo lo yevaréš.
Despu'és ke lo lavareš,   mi korona le meteréš.
Kazaréš al Don Virğile   kon la ṣovrina del rey.
28 Y'a kazan al Don Virğile   kon la ṣovrina de 'el rey.

Heading: rom[ans]a.
1a *et passim*   *MS*: aldon Virğile, 'eldon V., deldon V.
1b   *MS*: 'enlos.
5b   *MS*: konsí.
8a   *MS*: vestira.
9b   mužer: *There is an ink mark following the* reš *which could represent a* yodh
   (=*a paragogic* e?).
11b   *MS*: 'enprezo.
18b, 27b, 28b   *MS*: konla.
21b   *MS*: 'enestas.

2. *Rico Franco* (MP 85)

’I ’una ’iža tyene ’el rey   ’i no la troka ni por ’oro, ni por ’oro,
ni por aver,
¡Ğanim ayy!
ni por azyenda menuda   ke no se konta ’en ’un mes, mes,
¡ Ğanim ayy!
ṣino la metyyó al ğu’ego,   al ğu’ego del ašedrés.
¡ Ğanim ayy!
Ğugan ’unos, ğugan ’otros,   ’i ninguno no la gané.
¡ Ğanim ayy!
5 Ğugó ’el moriko franko   ’i lu’ego la ganó.
¡ Ğanim ayy!
Blanka Ninyy’a ke ’esto veríy’a,   a yyorar ’enpeṣaríy’a.
¡ Ğanim ayy!
— ¿De ké yoráš, Blanka Ninyy’a,   de ké yoráš, Blanka Flor?
¡ Ğanim ayy!
Si yoráš por ’el vu’estro padre,   ’el mi gizandero ’es.
¡ Ğanim ayy!
Si yoráš por la vu’estra madre,   la mi lavandera ’eš.
¡ Ğanim ayy!
10 Si yoráš por vu’estros ’ermanos,   yo los matí a todos tres.
¡ Ğanim ayy!
—No yoro por padre ni madre,   ni por mis ’ermanos tres.
¡ Ğanim ayy!
Yoro yo por la mi ventura,   kižera saver kén ’es.
¡Ğanim ayy!
—Si yoráš por vu’estra ventura,   de delantre la tenéš.
¡Ğanim ayy!
—Dešme ’un poko ’el vu’eṣtro kuğiyo,   ’el kuğiyiko del ağiprés,
¡Ğanim ayy!
15 a kortar de mis kaveyos   de ’un palmo asta tres,
¡Ğanim ayy!
a ma[n]dárselos al mi padre,   ke vey’a mi ventura kén ’es.
¡Ğanim ayy!
’El moriko, por ser loko,   por la kağa se lo dyyo.
¡Ğanim ayy!
18 La muğağa, por ser sezuda,   al korasón se lo apuntó.
¡Ğanim ayy!

4b   gané *seems to have been altered to* ganó.
6b   *MS:* ’en peṣaríy’a.
11a   ni madre *repeated.*
16a   *There is a worm hole in the MS.*

3. *Silvana* (MP 98)

[Paseáva]se Silbana ¡amán!　por 'un verǧel ke teníy'a,
vigu'ela de 'oro 'en su mano ¡amán!　'i tanyer ke la tanyí'a.
Si byen tanye, mežo[r] tembla, ¡amán!　mežor romanṣes dezíy'a.
'El rey su padre ke la syente, ¡amán!　de 'elyy'a se namoraríya.
5　—Suvirés akí, Silvana, ¡amán!　subirés akí, mi 'iža.
¡Ké byen pareséš, Silbana ¡amán!　kon vestidos de kada díy'a!
más ke la reyna tu madre, ¡amán!　ke los yeva de seda fina.
Si vos plazyera, Silbana, ¡amán!　de ser vos amiga míy'a.
—¡Plazerme, dišo, 'el mi padre, ¡amán!　plazerme, dezkortezíy'a!
10　'I las penas del 'enfermo ¡amán!　ṣé kén las paṣaríy'a.
—Yo las paṣaré, mi 'iža, mi byen,　yo las paṣaré 'en vida,
ke 'en mu'erte no 'eš maravíy'a. ¡Amán!　—'I dešéšme 'ir alos
　　　　　　　　　　　　　　　　　banyyos.
'I dešésme ['ir] alos banyyos, ¡amán!　alos banyyos de aguas
　　　　　　　　　　　　　　　　　fríyas,
a lavarme 'i 'entrenṣarme ¡amán!　'i mudarme 'una kamiza,
15　komo azíy'a la reyna ¡amán!　kuando kon 'el rey dormíy'a.
Y'a partíy'a Ṣilvana, ¡amán!　ya ṣe parte, y'a ṣe 'iva.
—Ǧuṣtiṣyy'a, Ṣenyyor del mundo, ¡amán!　ke 'en la tyera non
　　　　　　　　　　　　　　　　　avíy'a.
'Oído la avíy'a la madre, ¡amán!　de altaṣ tores de ariva:
—¡Válgame 'el Dyyo del syelo ¡amán!　'i tambyén la madre
　　　　　　　　　　　　　　　　　míy'a!
20　Ṣuviréš akí, Silvana, mi byen,　suvirés akí, mi 'iža.
Kontéšme vu'estros 'enožos ¡amán!　'i vu'estra mala 'enkonyí'a,
ke 'en ṣupyendo las vedrades, mi byen,　todo se aremedyarí'a,
ke 'en la mu'erte non ayy remedyyo, mi byen,　'en la vida munǧo
　　　　　　　　　　　　　　　　　avíy'a.
—'Un padre ke a mí keríy'a, ¡amán!　de amores me akometíy'a.
25　—Non yoredeš voš, Silvana, mi byen,　non yoredeš vos, mi 'iža.
'Enprestéšme vu'estros vestidos, ¡amán!　los ke vestíš kada díy'a.
'Iré por vos alos banyyos, ¡amán!　alos banyyos de aguas fríyas.
'I arogéšle a vu'estro padre ¡amán!　ke kandela non ṣendyera.
Y'a ṣe partíy'a Ṣilvana, ¡amán!　ya ṣe 'iva, ke y'a veníy'a.
30　Al 'eskuro fu'ese andada, ¡amán!　'en kama del rey arodiada.
'I toda la noǧe, toda, ¡amán!　'el bu'en rey non la dormíy'a,
'esklamando: —¡'Ésta Silbana!, ¡amán!　y'amando ala su 'iža.
Kuando vino ala manyyana, ¡amán!　byen '[o'i]réš lo ke dezíy'a:
—¡Mal ayy'a 'en ti, Ṣilvana, ¡amán!　'i la madre ke a ti paríy'a!
35　'Este ku'erpo de Silvana ¡amán!　'era de mužer parida.
De ayy'í ṣaltó la madre: ¡amán!　—¡'I byen ayy'a 'en ti, Silvana!

¡ 'I byen ayy'a 'en ti, Silvana, ¡amán!   'i la madre ke a ti paríy'a!
38 Ke 'es 'esto, Silvana, mi byen,   kazada tú mereṣíyas.

1a   *Right-hand corner of the leaf is torn.*
1b   *MS:* vergel.
3a   mežo[r]: *There is a blot on the MS.*
16b *MS:* yaṣe.
17b ke 'en *is repeated in passing from one folio to the next.*
23b *MS:* 'enla.
32b *MS:* y'a mando.
33b '[o'i]réš: *There is a blot on the MS.*
34a, 36b, 37a   *MS:* 'enti.

4. *La infanta deshonrada* (MP 106)

Parida 'está la 'infanta,   parida 'está de 'una 'iža.
Del myedo del rey ṣu padre,   ṣe 'izo dela ḥazina;
mandar ayyamar al konde,   al konde ṣu namorado:
—¿ Ké aremoṣ, 'el bu'en konde,   'i kon 'esta kriyatura ?
5 —Para [s]u mal y'a ayy remedyyo;   para ti, va, búškatelo.
—Toméš punta de vu'eṣtra alda,   la kriyatura yevaráš.
'I 'en medyyo del kamino,   kon 'el rey 'eskontraríy'a:
— ¿ Ké yevavaš, 'el bu'en konde,   'en punta dela tu alda ?
—Almendrikaṣ, 'el bu'en rey,   gustižo de 'una prenyyada.
10 —Dešme 'unaṣ dos, 'el bu'en konde,   para mi 'iža la 'infanta,
ke la tengo muy ḥazina,   ke la agu'a no me le paṣa.
—No le pu'edo dar, 'el bu'en rey,   ke me laṣ dyeron kontadaṣ.
'Estaṣ palavraṣ dizyendo,   la kriyatura yorava.
—Tra'isyyón 'izisteš, konde,   kon mi 'iža la 'infanta.
15 'Unoṣ dezíyan:—Mataldo;   'otroṣ dezíyan:—Kazaldo.
16 'I y'a kazan al bu'en konde   kon ṣu 'iža la 'infanta.

Heading: romanṣa.
5a   [s]u: s *obscured by an ink blot.*
7a   *MS:* 'enmedyyo.
7b   *MS:* kon'el.
8a   yevavaš *altered to* yevavaṣ.
14b *MS:* konmí.
16b *MS:* konṣu.

5. *El encuentro del padre* (MP 125)

Kaminando por altas mares,   navegí kon 'una fortuna.
Kayí 'en tyeras aženas,   'onde non me konoṣíyan,
'onde non kantava gayyo,   ni menos kanta gayina,
'onde 'el lovo brameava   'i la le'ona reṣpondíy'a,
5 'onde no ayy aguas fríyas,   ni menos aguas yeladas.
Por ayy'í paṣaron doze kondes,   los grandes de 'estaṣ víyas:
—¿ Ké bušká[š] akí, manṣevo,   tan ṣolo por estas víyas?
—Buško yo a 'un 'ermano   'i 'un 'ermano ke teníy'a.
—Dešme senyyaleṣ del ṣu ku'erpo.   Ṣenyyales del ṣu ku'erpo
daríy'a:
10 —Alto 'era komo 'un pino,   dereǧo komo la fleǧa.
Anyyos teníy'a veynte 'i kuatro   'i la barva roša teníy'a.
—¡Aḥ! 'Este manṣevo tan 'ermozo   al pozo lo 'eǧaríyan.
13 Tantas amarguras vide,   más 'i más son las de agora.

Heading: romansa.
7a   *MS seems to be faded. Only the diacritic mark over the* šin *is visible.*

A1. *Virgilios* (vv. 1–16)
(J.N.U.L., MS Heb. 8⁰ 2946, fol. 19 v⁰)

A1. *Virgilios* (vv. 17–28)
(J.N.U.L., MS Heb. 8° 2946, fol. 20 r°)

A2. *Rico Franco* (vv. 1–13)
(J.N.U.L., MS Heb. 8⁰ 2946, fol. 18 vᵒ)

A2. *Rico Franco* (vv. 14–18)
(J.N.U.L., MS Heb. 8⁰ 2946, fol. 19 r⁰)

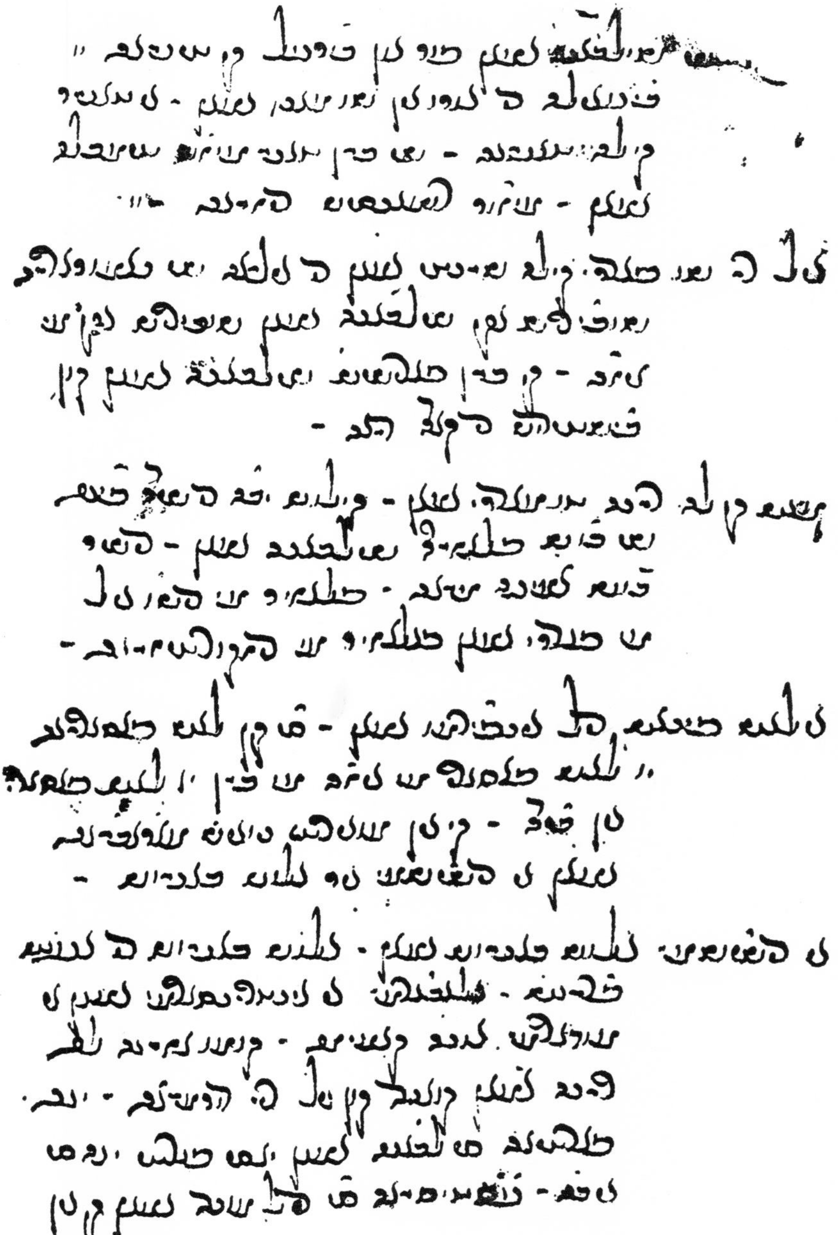

[Handwritten text in Hebrew/Judeo-Spanish script — four stanzas]

A3. *Silvana* (vv. I–I7)
(J.N.U.L., MS Heb. 8° 2946, fol. 5 v°)

A3. *Silvana* (vv. 17–33)
(J.N.U.L., MS Heb. 8° 2946, fol. 6 r°)

A3. *Silvana* (vv. 34–38)
(J.N.U.L., MS Heb. 8⁰ 2946, fol. 6 v⁰)

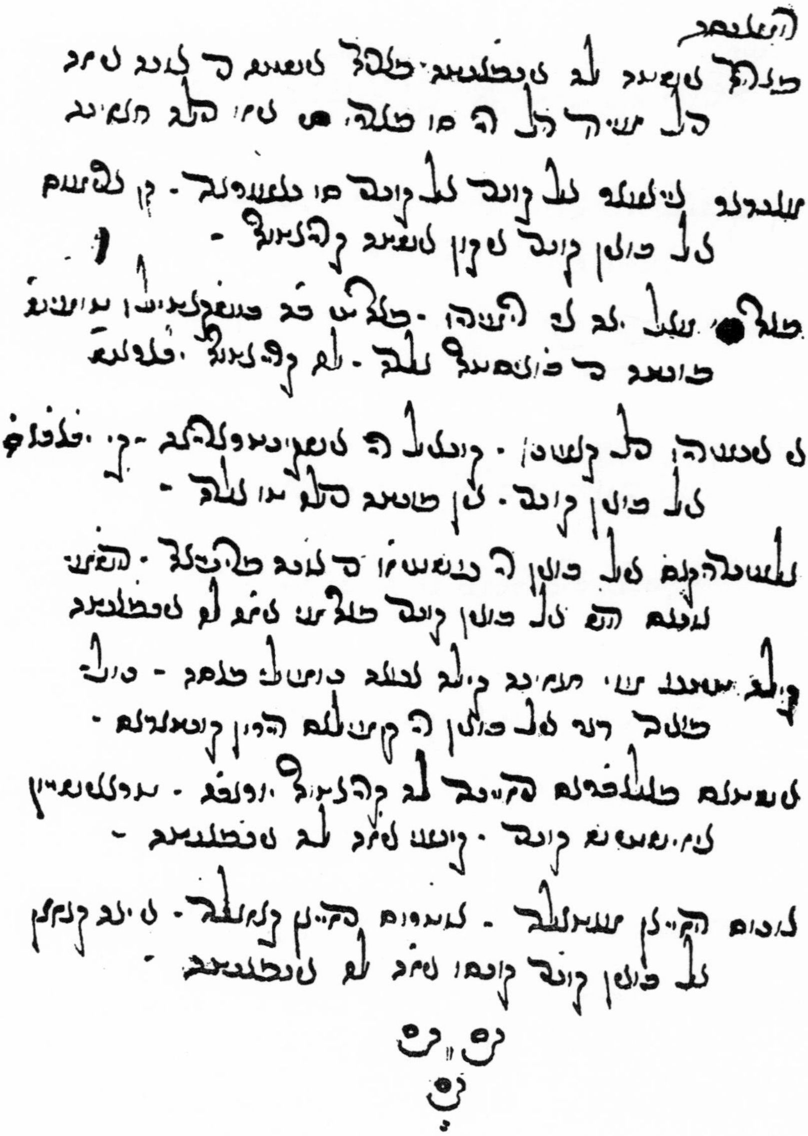

A4. *La infanta deshonrada*
(J.N.U.L., MS Heb. 8⁰ 2946, fol. 22 v⁰)

A5. *El encuentro del padre*
(J.N.U.L., MS Heb. 8º 2946, fol. 17 rº)

B.

KALMI BARUCH'S "SPANISH BALLADS OF THE
BOSNIAN JEWS" (1933)

K almi Baruch—scholar, teacher, and cultural leader—belonged to a generation of progressive Balkan Sephardim who took upon themselves the task of adapting the intellectual life of their communities to the patterns of Western European civilization.[a] Yet, in Baruch's case, this mission of cultural modernization was not inimical to the affectionate cultivation and close, scientific scrutiny of the language, folk literature, and ancient traditions of his people.

Born in Sarajevo at the very end of the nineteenth century, Kalmi Baruch finished high school there in 1917. After taking part in the First World War and suffering through two years as a prisoner of war in Russia, he returned to Yugoslavia to study at Zagreb. Later he undertook more advanced training in Vienna, Berlin, Paris, and Madrid, where his contacts with Spanish scholars made a lasting contribution to his intellectual formation. In 1923 he completed his Vienna doctoral dissertation, *Der Lautstand des Judenspanischen in Bosnien*. Eventually, Baruch returned as a teacher to Sarajevo, where he worked tirelessly—studying, writing, and contributing creatively to the cultural life of the community. Western students of Sephardic culture—among them, Cynthia Crews and Max Leopold Wagner—benefited significantly in their research efforts from his generous and enthusiastic collaboration, either through correspondence or *in situ* at Sarajevo.[b] The fruits of Baruch's intense literary and scholarly activities saw print in Serbo-Croatian and Judeo-Spanish in local newspapers and journals[c]—among them, significantly for us, the *Jevrejski Glas*—and also in Spanish and French in publications of international scope, such as the *Revista de Filología Española*,[d] the *Festschrift* for Salomon Rosanes,[e] and the *Revue Internationale des Études Balkaniques*.[f] Spanish literature, on one hand, and Hispano-

a. See Samuel Kamhi, "Dr. Kalmi Baruh," *Spomenica*, pp. 289–293. On the Europeanization of the Balkans and of the Sephardic colonies in particular, see Joseph Nehama's sensitive appraisal in our *Judeo-Spanish Ballad Chapbooks of Y. A. Yoná*, Introduction, *n.* 18.

b. Cf. Crews, *Recherches*, pp. 12–13.

c. See Kamhi, p. 290. For a Judeo-Spanish essay by Baruch on "La lingua de los sefardim," see Wagner, *Caracteres*, pp. 105–113. Cf. also pp. 58–60.

d. His "El judeo-español de Bosnia," *RFE*, XVII (1930), 113–151, is an indispensable contribution to the study of Eastern Judeo-Spanish.

e. "La obra judeo-española del Professor Max Leopold Wagner," *Iubileen' Sbornik' Š. Rozanes': Sēfer ha-Yôbēl lĕ-Ḥag ha-Šibʿîm* (Sofia, 1933), pp. 30–36.

f. "Les juifs balkaniques et leur langue," *Revue Internationale des Études Balkaniques*, I (Belgrade, 1935), 511–517.

Sephardic cultural and linguistic ties, on the other, constituted the chief foci of his writings.[g] His Serbo-Croatian article, "Španske romanse bosanskih Jevreja" ("Spanish Ballads of the Bosnian Jews"),[h] which we have translated and reedited here, not only offers an excellent collection of texts but also constitutes the first and only systematic survey of the Bosnian Sephardic ballad tradition to appear in print.

In 1943, faced with the threatening anti-Jewish activities of Croatian Fascists, Kalmi Baruch was forced to flee Sarajevo. He was taken prisoner by the Nazis in Cetinje, a small Montenegran town where he had sought refuge. When victorious Allied troops reached the death-camp at Bergen-Belsen in the Spring of 1945, Kalmi Baruch— though wracked by typhus and extenuated by torture, hard labor, and hunger—was still clinging to life. He died only two days after the camp's liberation.

In editing the ballad texts in "Španske romanse bosanskih Jevreja," we have strictly maintained Baruch's standardized Castilian orthography. Accents and the dieresis have, however, been supplied where needed, and we have freely modified the capitalization and punctuation. We have also numbered the verses and have identified each ballad with a conventional title and, where possible, with its number in Menéndez Pidal's "Catálogo" (MP). We have modified the numeration of the footnotes between nn. 1 and 5; from that point on the original numeration has been preserved. Material we have added is enclosed in brackets. The words "ballad" and "romance," in free alternation, render Baruch's Serbo-Croatian romansa. The following minor matters should also be noted: 9.19a: originally lamareis; 9.19b: originally que te escape; 11.13a: originally ala buba; 16.4a: originally Gritó da; 16.6b, 8b: originally hija una; 9.17, 11.17 and 19, 14.6: Baruch considers 2d hemistichs as 1st hemistichs.

g. Kalmi Baruch's writings on Hispanic subjects were brought together posthumously and reprinted under the title Eseji i članci iz španske književnosti svjetlost (Sarajevo, 1952). This volume includes his ballad essay (pp. 183–204).

h. "Španske romanse bosanskih Jevreja," Godišnjak izdaju La Benevolencia i Potpora (Sarajevo-Belgrade, 1933), pp. 272–288.

SPANISH BALLADS OF THE BOSNIAN JEWS

by Kalmi Baruch

Romances are frequently discussed among us. There are even some who have written enthusiastically about this poetic antiquity preserved and cultivated in the homes of the Sephardic Jews. From conversations with acquaintances, I have learned that opinions concerning the value of the *romances* are divided. Some people see them as an expression of primitive poetry, and yet, precisely for that reason, of a sincere poetry, inspired by the most tender feelings—still cherished by the Sephardic Jews—toward a remote history and a not-so-distant past. Others listen to the *romances* with a smile, not always free from an element of scorn, for they see in them a part of our folk literature that is, in any event, doomed to disappear.

It is not our concern to decide which of these prevailing views is closer to the truth, particularly since most of the people involved treat the subject on the basis of personal prejudices rather than according to scholarly criteria. We shall approach the subject in another way and with a different goal in mind. We shall try to show the connections that may exist between the *romances* still surviving among the Sephardic Jews of Bosnia and the rich and variegated traditional *Romancero* of the Iberian Peninsula, where the ballad originated and whence it spread, on one hand, to the Spanish republics of South America and, on the other, to the colonies of Spanish Jews in Morocco and the East.

Research carried out during the last decades has brought to light the survival of this kind of Spanish folk poetry in all those countries where the Spanish language is still in use today. Our purpose, then, is 1) to determine the degree to which the Hispanic *romance* has been preserved in Bosnia and in what form; 2) to study the creative power of the Bosnian Sephardic community and its capacity to add new ballads to its inherited treasury; and, finally, 3) to identify those other songs that are called *romances* simply because they are sung in Spanish by Sephardic Jews, though in form and spirit they have nothing in common with the great Spanish *Romancero* tradition.

Before beginning our discussion, I would like to stress that this material was generously presented to me by Mrs. Laura Papo, a well-known figure in the community and undoubtedly one of the outstanding connoisseurs of the Sephardic oral tradition in Bosnia. I shall also, in part, make use of the *romances* which I had the good fortune to hear in my own social circle.

I

I am certain that it is clear to our readers that we must say a few introductory words about the origins and development of the *romance* in general, before we get to our specific subject, inasmuch as people here have little background in such matters. Scholars who investigated foreign literatures became acquainted with this subject through the study of Romanticism. The Romanticists, especially the Germans (Herder, J. Grimm, Lachmann, for example), were the first to call attention to the unique poetic values and importance of the Spanish *Romancero*. They saw in it the living remnants of the Spanish folk epic. And in this they were correct, although their conclusions concerning the epics of other European nations (Greece, France, Germany) were proven wrong after long years of research in that field. For the most part, they believed that the folk epic was a spontaneous and unsophisticated creation of a whole people. They felt that the great epics, like the *Iliad*, the *Odyssey*, the French heroic epic, the *Niebelungenlied*, derived from short poems and they tried to prove this point with the example of the Spanish *romances*. They also maintained that the famous twelfth-century *Poema del Cid* was composed from a whole series of previously existing ballads. In Spain, A. Durán supported this thesis. Later on, in the second half of the nineteenth century, a new theory was propounded on completely different principles. A famous authority on the *Romancero*, M. Milá y Fontanals, stated that a *romance* was, in the first place, the work of a single author and not "of the whole people"; that *romances* were created for the noble class and the knights; and that they had their origin in the longer epic poems.

This point of view was generally accepted by Don Ramón Menéndez Pidal, the distinguished philologist and greatest living authority on Spanish folk poetry. Above all, he maintained that *romances*, far from being spontaneous, unsophisticated creations, were the "fruits of literary ambitions" and "the end result of an aristocratic or learned style." *Romances*, he thought, were fragments of longer poems which had existed in an earlier time and, perhaps also simultaneously with the *romances*. Such a long poem was the one concerning the folk hero known as the Cid; traces of other long epics were found by Menéndez Pidal in the famous *Crónica General de España*, the compilation of which is associated with King Alfonso the Wise in the second half of the thirteenth century.[1]

1. For all of this see R. Menéndez Pidal, "Poesía popular y poesía tradicional en la literatura española," *El Romancero: Teorías e investigaciones* (Madrid, [1928]), pp. 7–60.

During a period of some three decades, Menéndez Pidal has been authoritatively investigating the problems of the Spanish *Romancero*, on the basis of written sources and, in particular, of the living tradition of all Spanish-speaking countries. By studying numerous variants of the same *romance* (for some of them, he claims, there are 200 to 300 variant versions in his collection), he has demonstrated that these fragments of longer poems had, as was only natural, gradually undergone changes in the memory of individuals and in various geographical regions and that the objective, narrative elements of the *romances* were slowly forgotten, while subjective, sentimental features were added. Thus, both in spirit and style, the epic fragments began to change: their character, in the beginning purely epico-narrative, had now become epico-lyrical in nature. In spite of the internal changes undergone by the Spanish folk epics (the medieval *cantares de gesta*) in the process of their transformation into the still surviving *romance*, their original metrical form has been preserved. The *romance* consists of a series of sixteen-syllable verses with assonant rhyme.

One of the basic characteristics of Spanish folk poetry is its traditionalism. The oral as well as the written tradition presents historical events and personages in a continuum, so that the old epic themes— King Rodrigo, the last Gothic king; the Cid; the legendary Bernardo del Carpio; the Seven Princes of Lara—were absorbed by the *romances* and were adapted to the spirit of the times. These same themes were to appear again in the Spanish theater of the sixteenth and seventeenth centuries. In addition to the above-mentioned national themes, figures from classical antiquity, from the Carolingian cycle, and from medieval chivalric novels were also treated.

In general, the *romances* that are still current today originated in the fifteenth century and some few of them in the fourteenth century; they reached full bloom in the sixteenth century. The first extensive collection of *romances* was printed in Antwerp. It is known today among scholars as the *Cancionero de romances, sin año*, because its year of publication was not mentioned. This collection must have been published prior to 1550, since during that year Martín Nucio, the original editor, printed a second edition of that invaluable literary monument.[2] Nucio had undoubtedly collected *romances* in manuscript

2. *Cancionero de romances impreso en Amberes sin año*, Edición facsímil con una introducción por R. Menéndez Pidal, Madrid, 1914. [The conventional English term *broadsheets*, or *broadsides*, does not really correspond exactly to Baruch's *zasebni tabaci* 'separate sheets', nor to the Spanish *pliegos sueltos* 'unbound quires,' a kind of primitive chapbook. For a discussion of the exact distinction between these terms see E. M. Wilson's penetrating review of C. Colin Smith's *Spanish Ballads* (Oxford, 1964), *BHS*, XLII (1965), 186–187, and A. Rodríguez-Moñino, *Poesía y cancioneros (Siglo XVI)* (Madrid, 1968), pp. 31–32.]

form, in primitive printed broadsheets (*pliegos sueltos*), and probably also in versions that were sung by Spaniards living in Holland at that time. During the same year another rather large collection appeared in Zaragoza, and in subsequent years several other similar *cancioneros* were published, all of which indicates the great popularity enjoyed by this kind of poetry in Spain. It is well known that the *romance* form was cultivated by almost all the great writers of the Classical period, among them Lope de Vega, Quevedo, and others.

II

Let us now investigate the *romance* tradition among the Sephardic Jews. On this subject, we are fortunate once again in having an authoritative work by the Spanish scholar Ramón Menéndez Pidal.[3] Taking into account previously published collections,[4] Menéndez Pidal classified about 150 *romances* from areas where the Sephardic Jews lived, indicating relationships and differences between these ballads and those printed in earlier collections or still sung in Spain.

As to the age of the Jewish *romances*, it is evident that the Jews, exiled from Spain in 1492, took with them a large ballad repertoire. Travel diaries indicate that, in their new surroundings in the East, the Jews managed to maintain contacts with their brethren on the Iberian Peninsula. Moreover, it was precisely in Antwerp—where the two previously mentioned ballad collections were published—that many Jews who escaped from the Inquisition had settled and where they maintained a network of trade relations with all the major cities of Europe. It is not impossible that a certain number of *romances* could have reached the East through such channels. In his study of the Judeo-Spanish *Romancero*, Menéndez Pidal quotes several ballads dealing with events which took place subsequent to 1492 (*Muerte del Duque de Gandía, Muerte del Príncipe Don Juan*, the latter from

3. "Catálogo del romancero judío-español," reprinted in the above-mentioned book, *El Romancero*, pp. 101–183. Because this work is often mentioned in the present article, we will refer to it as *Catál.* [We have replaced Baruch's abbreviations with those used elsewhere in the present book and in our other publications. Thus, instead of Baruch's "*Catál.*" and "REJ," we use "MP" and "Danon."]

4. Abraham Danon, "Recueil des romances judéo-espagnoles chantées en Turquie," published in *Revue des Études Juives*, 1896; [M.] Menéndez y Pelayo, *Antología de [poetas] líricos castellanos*, X (1900). [Baruch owned the off-print of Danon's collection (Paris: A. Durlacher, 1896), whose title page reads "des romances," instead of "de romances" as on p. 102 of the original article (and also p. 3 of the off-print). Baruch uses the off-print's pagination in *n.* 7. He probably did not own the *Antología*; he reproduces the error of *El Romancero*, p. 102, *n.* 3: "Antología de líricos."]

Morocco and Edirne). This fact, as well as the documentary proof of the exiled Jews' sixteenth- and seventeenth-century contacts with Spain, leads him to conclude: "The majority of Jewish *romances* are medieval, but not all of them."[5] Regarding the value of its individual texts as a complement to variant versions surviving in Spain, Menéndez Pidal considers the Judeo-Spanish ballad tradition "antigua y venerable más que la de cualquier región donde se habla nuestro idioma."[6]

The contacts between the Jewish centers and Spain were, naturally, not very close. It is therefore not surprising that in the ballads' land of origin there are many texts, mostly of a later date, of which there is no record among the Jews. At the same time, a significant number of *romances*, not known on the Peninsula, exist among the Sephardim. These are mostly of Biblical inspiration and, consequently, derive from the living Jewish tradition.[6a] There is, however, another kind of ballad, of completely different origin and character, about which we shall speak when we begin to analyze the Bosnian *romances*. In any event, such texts show that, for the *sefardí* and his community the *romance* was the ideal vehicle for the poetic expression of sentiment. Its verse form and rhythm enabled it to endure from generation to generation, to such a degree that one must really admire its great vitality.

We have all taken part in social functions that were accompanied by the singing of *romances* until not so long ago: female singers with tambourines performed regularly at weddings, at the festivities following a circumcision, or when someone moved into a new home. Most extraordinary is a Hebrew passage cited by Abraham Danon, which bears witness to the fact that a *romance* melody was even used in a Hebrew synagogal hymn written by the poet Israel Nagiara. In 1600 this religious poet published in Venice a book of songs entitled *Zemirot Jisrael*, in which he used the initial verses of various *romances* as headings to indicate the melody to which the Hebrew hymns (*piyyutim*) were to be sung.[7]

5. MP, p. 120.

6. MP, p. 101.

6a. [Baruch's supposition should be modified in the light of what we say in "Christian Elements," pp. 24–25, *nn.* 11–12. See also our review of M. Alvar, *Poesía tradicional de los judíos españoles* (Mexico City, 1966), *RPh*, XXII (1968–1969), 235–242: p. 237.]

7. Danon translated the following quotation from the Hebrew: "On doit réprouver quelques poésies qui commencent par des mots imités de l'espagnol. De ce nombre est le chant: מרומי על מה עם רם הומה composé sur l'air des vers: *muero-me mi alma, ay muero-me*, dont l'auteur ignorait que ce procédé est abominable, parce qu'il rappelle à celui qui chante ces vers des souvenirs luxurieux.... Cependant, j'ai remarqué que l'auteur de l'ouvrage *Zemiroth*

Of all the Hispano-Jewish communities, the *romance* is best preserved in Morocco. The Jews of that region were the closest to Spain,
whence they could easily receive those ballads created in the sixteenth and seventeenth centuries. According to Menéndez Pidal, his
collection of Moroccan *romances* contains texts which are still anima-
ted by the old heroic spirit of the Spanish epics. Moreover, as far as
I can gather from the collections I know, this is also the only Jewish
community which has preserved three examples of the so-called *romances moriscos*.[7a] These are ballads created in the fifteenth century,
during the final battles between Arabs and Spaniards. One of them
begins as follows:

> Mañanita era, mañana,   al tiempo que alboreaba,
> gran fiesta hacían los moros   en la bella de Granada.
> Arrevuelven sus caballos   y van jugando la danza.
> Aquel que amiga tenía,   allí se la congraciaba;
> y el que no la tenía,   procuraba de alcanzarla.[8]

III

Let us now turn to the ballads which are still alive today among
the Sephardic Jews of Bosnia. First of all we must stress that they
are fewer in number than those of Danon's collection and much less
numerous than those received by Menéndez Pidal from Morocco. Both
of these collections were, of course, formed some thirty years ago and
I assume that in Bosnia, as elsewhere, some ballads have been lost as
a result of the general decline of the living oral tradition. However,
it seems probable that many of the very interesting examples published in these two collections either never existed in Bosnia or else
were forgotten long ago. Historical *romances* which tell of the folk

Jisraël (Nag'ara) ne s'en fait aucun scrupule.... Pendant mon séjour à Damas,
je le lui ai reproché...." (Danon, p. 4 [= p. 103]). [Rabbi Herbert C. Dobrinsky
and Dr. Herman P. Salomon were kind enough to provide us with pertinent
information about this Hebrew *incipit*. It is from an unidentified hymn with
no known biblical source. The verse means 'An exalted people longs for the
heights of the world.' More important than meaning, however, is the fact that
it approximates the phonetic structure of the Spanish verse. Dr. Salomon, who
is now completing an article on this and similar Hebrew-Spanish puns to be
published in the *American Sephardi*, called our attention to a brief discussion of
this linguistic phenomenon in E. Aguilar and D. A. De Sola, *The Ancient Mel-
odies of the Liturgy of the Spanish and Portuguese Jews* (London, 1857), p. 14,
n. 12.]

7a. [Read: *romances fronterizos*. However, see our "Dos romances fronterizos
en la tradición sefardí oriental."]

8. MP, p. 129. [Concerning these verses, see our article "*La sanjuanada*:
¿ Huellas de una *ḫarǧa* mozárabe en la tradición actual ?" (to appear in *NRFH*).]

hero, *El Cid*; of the tragic death of the Seven Princes of Lara, who were cruelly sent into unequal battle against the Moors by their vengeful uncle Ruy Velázquez; and even one ballad concerning the legendary hero Bernardo del Carpio have, for example, been found in Morocco and, in some cases, also in Salonika. It is true that even in these Jewish communities the historical ballads cannot be compared in number to the nonhistorical ones. However, it is at least possible to assume that formerly there were many more historical themes and that they have since been forgotten. In Bosnia, on the other hand, I have never heard any of them. The small number of historical ballads known among the Jews and the fact that, in some cases, they have been completely forgotten can, I think, be explained by saying that probably the events, characters, and geographic names mentioned in these ballads disappeared long ago from the memory of the Sephardic Jews, who have lived for centuries now without any connection with Spain, the scene of all the events with which the *Romancero* is concerned.[8a] The Jews have preserved ballads dealing with the universal themes of human existence and also various others which are novelesque in content, referring to no specific time or place and corresponding to the views and imagination of a primitive Eastern people.

If we bear in mind that here we are dealing with a form of popular poetry which has been kept alive primarily among people of little or no formal education—if, furthermore, we do not forget that the *romances* have never been written down or used as a vehicle for any kind of literary activity—then it will become clear to us why they are now in such a decadent state in Bosnia. Here we find the hybridism of two or more ballads, the transposition of various verses, changes in assonance, etc. The singer may forget details or lack the intelligence to comprehend the inner threads of the ballad's story; finally, as a result of a latent but constant deterioration of the Spanish language among the Jews, we find frequent substitutions of words and concepts and a breakdown in rhythm and verse structure. We will point out these deficiencies as we go along. In order to render the analysis of our material as systematic as possible, we will classify the ballads according to their principal themes.

First of all, several *romances* on the theme of faithful love, galvanized by great suffering and hardship, are current in Bosnia. Such is the ballad of *Don Vergile*, recorded long ago in Spain and also known among the Jews of Morocco and the Near East:[8b]

8a. [On the erosion of toponyms and personal names in the Eastern Judeo-Spanish *Romancero*, see our "Dos romances fronterizos," p. 91, *n.* 7. See also *nn.* 11, 12 below.]

8b. MP, pp. 144–145.

[1. *Virgilios* (MP 46)]

Mal grado se iba Don Vergile   por los palacios del rey,
por amar a una muchacha   que se llamaba Zaïdé.
Ni más alta, ni más baja,   sobrina era del rey.
Tanto era el mal que hacía,   que en oídos del rey fue.
5   —Aquí, aquí, la mi gente,   los que del mi pan coméis.
Tomadlo a Don Vergile,   a la cárcel lo metéis.
Ni le daréis de comer,   ni le daréis agua a beber
y las llaves de la cárcel   a mí me las trairéis.
Pasan días, vienen días,   minguno demanda por él.
10 Su madre, la desdichada,   cada día lo iba a ver.
Y un día de los días,   a misa se fue el rey.
Diciendo estaba el rey la misa,   vido venir una mujer;
vestida iba de preto   de cabeza hasta los pies.
Preguntó el rey a su gente   quién era esta mujer.
15   —Madre es de Don Vergile,   que en la cárcel lo tenéis.
—Presto digamos la misa   y vamos a comer
y después que ya comimos,   a Don Vergile iremos a ver.
Saltó la reina y dijo: —Yo no comeré sin él.
—Pues que a la reina place   y a la mi gente también.
20   —Buenos días, Don Vergile.   —Buenos días, señor rey.
—¿Qué te parece, Don Vergile,   por las cárceles del rey?
—Bien me parece, señor rey,   bien me parece y bien es.
Cuando yo entrí en la cárcel,   barba me empezó a crecer.
Ahora, por mis pecados,   me se empezó a enblanquecer.
25 Siete años estó en la cárcel,   tres mancan para diez.
Pues que al señor rey le place,   los cumpliré todos tres.
—Por esta palabra, Don Vergile,   de la cárcel saliréis.
Aquí, aquí, la mi gente,   los que de mi pan coméis.
Tomadlo a Don Vergile,   de la cárcel lo quitaréis.
30 Lavadlo y arrapadlo,   vestidle paños de rey.
31 Después que lo vestiréis,   con Zaidé lo casaréis.

Some typical verses, which we also find in heroic ballads, indicate
the ancient, Spanish origin of this *romance*. For instance, the legendary
hero, Bernardo del Carpio, stubbornly refusing to yield to King Alfonso
the fortified city bearing his name, calls upon his soldiers in exactly
the same way as does the imaginary king in our ballad:

¡Aquí, aquí, los mis doscientos,   los que comedes mi pan![9]

9. R. Menéndez Pidal, *Flor nueva de romances viejos* ([Madrid], 1928), p. 92.
(This work is also frequently mentioned here and we will refer to it as *Flor*.)
[On the formula in question, see now Yoná, No. 1, *n*. 23.]

The father of Bernardo del Carpio, the Count of Saldaña, fell in love with the king's sister Jimena; the fruit of that love was Bernardo himself. Furious, the king throws the count into prison. The prisoner, complaining that his son has done nothing to obtain his freedom, uses the following words which we also find in our Bosnian *romance*:

> Cuando entré en este castillo   apenas entré con barba,
> y agora por mis pecados   la veo crecida y blanca.[10]

The ballad of *La sirena*, as sung in Bosnia, represents a typical example of Oriental adaptation of an old and extremely popular Spanish *romance*. Its theme is the miraculous metamorphoses of persecuted lovers, a motif which also occurs frequently in European (Tristan) and in Eastern literature:

[2. *Conde Olinos* (MP 55)]

—Hija mía, mi querida,   vente una noche a mi odá,
Sentirás cantar hermoso   a la sirena de la mar.
—Sirena de mar, mi madre,   no cantó ni va cantar,
sino es un mancebico   que me quere alcanzar.
5 Cantará día y noche,   a mí no me alcanzará.
Esto que sintió su madre,   presto lo corrió a matar.
Y después que ya lo matan,   que lo echen a quemar,
y aquella cenicica,   que la echen a la mar.
Que de ahí sale la perla,   perla fina y buen coral.
10 Esto que sintió la hija,   presto lo corrió a escapar.
Ella se hizo una palomba,   a él lo hizo un gavilán.
Volan, volan, ¿ónde apozan?   A los konakes del pašá.
Allí se topó un espino   que non los dejaba gozar.
Volan, volan, ¿ónde apozan?   A los konakes del vezir.
15 Ahí se topó un espino   que no los dejaba vivir.

Menéndez Pidal reconstructed this ballad from numerous versions in his possession. In this reconstruction, the hero is *Conde Niño*; the heroine *la infanta*, who is reprimanded by her mother, the queen; and the time is "la mañana de San Juan."[11] In the Bosnian version, these aristocratic protagonists are simply replaced by "mancebico," "hija," "madre" and the time is also reduced to "una noche." The same thing happens in A. Danon's version from Edirne.[12] I will quote

10. *Flor*, p. 89.
11. *Flor*, p. 157.
12. Danon, No. 19.

the beautiful dénouement of the reconstructed text, so that we can perceive the aforementioned transformation of the Sephardic ballad, even though the changes concern mostly its external form, language, and locality:

> El murió a la media noche,   ella a los gallos cantar;
> a ella como hija de reyes   la entierran en el altar,
> a él como hijo de conde   unos pasos más atrás.
> De ella nació un rosal blanco,   dél nació un espino albar;
> crece el uno, crece el otro,   los dos se van a juntar;
> las ramitas que se alcanzan   fuertes abrazos se dan,
> y las que no se alcanzaban   no dejan de suspirar.
> La reina llena de envidia   ambos los mandó cortar;
> el galán que los cortaba   no cesaba de llorar.
> Della naciera una garza,   dél un fuerte gavilán;
> juntos vuelan por el cielo,   juntos vuelan par a par.

We will mention two more love ballads that are well known in Bosnia. One of them reminds us of the love-legend of Hero and Leander. I have not been able to find evidence that either of them was ever known in Spain:[12a]

[3. *Hero y Leandro* (MP 41)]

> Tres hermanicas (ellas) eran,   tres hermanicas (ellas) son.
> Las dos eran casadas,   la chica a la perdición.
>   ¡Ah, morenica y sabrosica y mi cara de flor!
> Su padre, por vergüenza,   a Francia la mandó.
> En medio de mares,   castillos le fraguó,
> 5   de piedra y de cal,   ventanas al derredor.
> Varón que esto sentía,   a nadar se echó,
> nadando y navegando,   llamando Cara-de-flor.
> Morena durmiendo,   la voz le conoció.
> 9   Le echó sus trenzados,   arriba lo asubió.

The next ballad, which is also recorded by Danon, probably originated in the East, for it is unknown to the Jews of Morocco:

12a. [Concerning the Hero and Leander theme in Spain, see now A. Alatorre, "Los romances de Hero y Leandro," reprinted from *Libro Jubilar de Alfonso Reyes* (Mexico City, 1956); F. Moya del Baño, *El tema de Hero y Leandro en la literatura española* (Murcia, 1966). On the origin of the Sephardic ballad, see our "New Collection," pp. 141–142 (No. 17).]

[4. *Choza del desesperado* (MP 140)]

Irme quero, la mi madre,   por los campos me iré.
Yerbesicas de los campos   por pan me las comeré.
Lágrimas de los mis ojos   por agua las beberé.
En medio de estos campos,   castillos me fraguaré.
5 Todo el que por ahí pasa,   arriba lo subiré.
El que conte los sus males;   yo los míos contaré.
Si los suyos son más grandes,   con paciencia los llevaré.
8 Si los míos son más grandes,   del castillo me echaré.

On the other hand, the following short ballad, concerning love between a princess and a harvest man, is well known in Spain:[13]

[5. *La princesa y el segador* (MP 108)]

El rey tiene una hija,   una hija regalada.
Metióla en altas torres,   por tenerla bien guardada.
Un día, de las calores,   aparece a la ventana.
Tomó cuchillo en mano   para mundar una manzana.
5 Por ahí pasaron segadores   que siegan trigo y cebada.
—Que mi acogéis el mi trigo   y mi cebada.
Si por aquí, no por ahí,   si por debajo de mis ventanas.
Segador que esto sentía,   ahí tomó la morada.
Mandóle el rey llamar su padre   con una de sus esclavas.
10 Camino de ocho días,   lo hizo en tres semanas.

Among other themes, seemingly the best preserved are those *romances* concerning the wife's faithfulness. *Arboleda,* one of the most famous Bosnian ballads, is widely diffused in all areas of the Iberian Peninsula.[14] It is also well known in other Eastern Jewish colonies.[15] We would say that this is generally one of the best preserved Bosnian ballads. Its story is complete and homogeneous; its verses and assonance are regular; the dialog between husband and wife is fluent and lively:

13. MP, No. 108.
14. MP, p. 150.
15. Danon, No. 17.

[6. *La vuelta del marido* (*i*) (MP 58)]

Arboleda, arboleda,   tan galana, tan gentil,
la raíz tiene de oro   y las ramas de marfil.
La más chica ramica   es una dama jarif,
peñando los sus trenzados   con su peine cristalín.
5 Por ahí pasó un caballero,   que semejava a Amadí.
—Así vivas caballero,   así el Dio vos deje vivir,
¿si vistéis al mi marido,   al mi marido, Amadí?
—Bien lo vide, bien lo conozco,   letra tengo para ti.
¿Cuánto dierais, la mi señora,   porque vo lo trujera aquí?
10 —Diera yo mis tres doblones   que me quedaron de Amadí.
—¿Cuánto dierais, la mi señora,   porque vos lo trujera aquí?
—Diera yo los tres trenzados   que me quedaron de Amadí.
—¿Cuánto dierais, la mi señora,   porque vos lo trujera aquí?
—Diera yo mis tres molinos   que me quedaron de Amadí.
15 El uno muele pimienta   y el otro ginquilí
y el más chico de ellos,   harina blanca para Amadí.
Diera yo mis tres hijicas   que me quedaron de Amadí.
La una mete la mesa   y la otra para servir
y la más chiquita de ellas,   para burlar y para reír.
20 —¿Dierais vos mi medio cuerpo   para que lo trujera aquí?
—Si yo do mi medio cuerpo,   ¿lo que le queda para Amadí?
22 —No pensés nada, mi señora,   yo soy el vuestro marido Amadí.

Another *romance* tells of the wife's fidelity in the face of temptation.
Both meter and diction are discordant, though the story is well told:

[7. *La vuelta del marido* (*á-a*)]

Asentada está la reina,   asentada en su vergel.
Agujica de oro en su mano,   ata bien i enfila perla.
Por ahí pasó un caballero   que a su marido asemejava.
—Así vivas, caballero,   así Dios vos dé bonanza,
5 ¿si vistéis a mi marido,   al Montesico de Francia?
—Bien lo vide, bien lo conozco,   letra en mi mano daba.
Me dijo que vos busquéis otro marido,   que él ya se buscó otra dama.
Esto que sintió la reina,   grito echaba dolorido,
que los cielos aborracaba   y la tierra retemblaba.
10 —No lloréis vos, la mi reina,   ni vos toméis dolor mucha.
Que yo soy vuestro marido,   el Montesico de Francia.
—Un mal hay a las mujeres   que en los hombres se confían.
13 Falsos son y mentirosos,   echados a la malicia.

Two ballads concerning the unfaithful wife also exist in Bosnia. They too are among the most popular. The first is *Andarleto*, one of the most widely diffused ballads among the Eastern Jews.[16] It is rare in Spain. The beginning is taken from some other *romance*, as is apparent in the change from *i-a* to *á-o* assonance. Its dénouement, after the queen's soliloquy, is beautiful and dynamic:

[8. *Landarico* (MP 82)]

A cazar el rey salía,   a cazar como solía.
Por irse a la caza,   onde la reina se ía.
Topó a la reina en cabellos,   que a peinar se los ía,
con su peine de oro en mano   y su espejo cristalín.
5 El rey, por burlar con ella,   con la verga le ha dado.
—State, state, Andarleto,   mi pulido enamorado.
Más te quiero y más te amo   que a el rey con su reinado.
Dos hijicos de ti tengo   y dos del rey, que son cuatro.
Los del rey van a la guerra   y los tuyos a mi lado.
10 Los del rey benean mula,   los tuyos mula y caballo.
Los del rey durmen en pluma   y los tuyos a mi lado.
Ella que aboltó la cara,   al rey se topó al lado.
—¡Perdón, perdón, mi señor rey,   por esto que vos he hablado!
Anoche a la media noche,   todo me lo fue soñando.
15 —Vos lo perdono, mi reina,   con la cabeza a mi lado.
—Andarleto, mi Andarleto,   mi pulido enamorado,
17 para mí topí remedio,   para vos andad buscando.

The other ballad on the same theme is also well known in the oral traditions of Spain, Chile, and Mexico.[17] It is very old. The person who interpreted this *romance* was betrayed here and there by his memory; one verse is even omitted altogether:

16. MP, p. 161.
17. *Flor*, pp. 151–154.

[9. *Bernal Francés* (MP 83)]

Labrando estaba la reina,   labrando en su vergel,
agujica de oro en mano,   escribanica de marfil.
Sintió batir a la puerta,   dejó todo y fue a abrir.
Dejó abierta media puerta   y media dejó por abrir.
5 A la entrada de la puerta,   se amataba el candil.
—¿Lo que es esto, el pelegrino?   No cale que hagas ansí.
—A mí me güelen los ojicos,   no los so cadir de abrir.
Tomólo mano por mano   y arriba lo subió.
Labóle pies y manos   con agua de turundjí.
10 Metióle mesa de oro,   onde el rey fue a comer.
Hácele cama de pluma   y onde el rey fue a dormir.
Ya pasó de la media noche,   no se abolta para aquí.
—¿Lo que es esto, el pelegrino?   No cale que hagas ansí.
Si tienes miedo del rey,   longe él está de aquí.
15 Ahí lo maten los leones   y las nuevas nos vengan aquí.
—Si llegare hasta la mañana,   te cortaré un buen vestir,
. . . .   la gargantera de kermezí.
Llamaréis al pelegrino   que te escape él a ti.
Llamaréis a padre y madre   que te escape[n] de aquí.
20 Ya llegó a la mañana   y le cortó un buen vestir.

The Bosnian variant is more superficial and less beautiful than the
one quoted by Menéndez Pidal (*La amiga de Bernal Francés*). This
is particularly apparent in the ending, which is the most important
part of the ballad. Here is how the above-mentioned version ends:

> Por regalo de mi vuelta   te he de dar rico vestir,
> vestido de fina grana   forrado de carmesí,
> gargantilla colorada   como en damas nunca vi;
> el collar será mi espada,   que tu cuello ha de ceñir.
> Nuevas irán al francés   que arrastre luto por ti.

Even in A. Danon's collection,[18] this ballad's dénouement is completely reworked.

The theme of the evil mother-in-law is extremely popular in the
primitive poetry of all peoples. Mrs. Laura Papo provided me with
this lone ballad, which is broken into uneven stanzas and adapted to
the melody. Its text is somewhat different from that of another ballad
on a similar theme recorded by Danon.[19] Here, the son attacks his

18. Danon, No. 24.
19. Danon, No. 9 [= *La mala suegra*].

mother with the intention of killing her because he has heard that she slandered her daughter-in-law (his own wife). Our Bosnian ballad ends with the death of the mother, who could not bear the news that her daughter had died in childbirth. And so, in Bosnia, two motifs merged: one about a mother-in-law "with a heart of stone" and another concerning motherly love. Danon's ballad has also lost the form of a *romance*. Moreoever, in Menéndez Pidal's materials there are two *romances* on the same theme. In one of them, mention is even made of *Don Buezo*[20] and therefore it is possible that both of them were confused in the memory of the Bosnian singer, who changed the hero's name to *Don Beso*. We will quote only one stanza:

[10. *Parto en lejas tierras* (MP 68)]

Alevantéis, Don Beso,
alevantéis, Don Beso,
que a la madre vuestra
a llamar la vayáis,
que a la Luz-del-día
el parto le tomaría.

Several other novelesque, nonhistorical ballads are known in Bosnia. There are various elements in them which are products of primitive folk-imagination. Over the centuries, these *romances* furnished a kind of secular recreation; in a sense, they fulfilled the function of "belles lettres" for the Sephardic Jews, who, otherwise, knew and cultivated only religious literature. These ballads deal with various imaginary events, journeys, imprisonments, women of unusual character, etc. We will give an account of them here and point out their relationship to other Spanish and Jewish versions of similar content.

The next ballad—which relates how a queen unexpectedly and under strange circumstances recognizes a slave-girl as her sister—is known among the Eastern Sephardim, in Morocco, and also in Spain.[21] This *romance* is also interesting as an example of the gradual deterio-

---

20. MP, p. 154 [= MP 69. Actually the ballads referred to: *El parto en lejas tierras* (MP 68), *La mala suegra castigada* (MP 69), and *La mala suegra* (MP 70) represent three quite independent text-types. The use of *Don Buezo* in both texts is coincidental. Needless to say, *El parto en lejas tierras* has not "lost the form of a *romance*." The six- and seven-syllable verses undoubtedly reflect its original form.]

21. MP, p. 145.

ration of the ballads' poetic value and of the character of their narratives in the course of time. Of the three variants that are known to me,[22] ours seems to be the least satisfactory:

[11. *Hermanas reina y cautiva* (MP 48)]

—Moricos, los mis moricos,   los que para Francia iban,
ellos buscan una esclava,   una esclava captiva.
No queren de vanda grande,   ni queren de vía y vía.
Ya se llevan una esclava   y al rey se la traían.
5 Ya se llevan una esclava   asigún demandarían.
La reina come pichones   y la esclava macarones.
La reina come gallinas,   la esclava taraínas.
La reina durme en plumas   y la esclava en las tablas.
Vino tiempo, pasa tiempo,   la reina queda preñada.
10 La reina queda preñada;   la esclava mejorada.
La reina parió una hija   y la esclava parió un hijo.
Las comadres fueron agudas,   trocaron las criaturas.
—A la nana, a la buba,   se durma esta criatura.
Tú creada de mis pechos,   non nacida de mi tripa.
15 Si eras mi criatura   ¿qué nombre yo te nombraba?
Yo te nombraba Marqueta,   nombre de una hermana mía,
. . . .   que es reina de alegría.
Un día de estos días,   pasó la reina por la cosina,
. . . .   le sentió esta cantica.
20 —Ven aquí tú, la mi esclava,   la mi esclava captiva.
Torna y canta esta cantica,   que mucho me agradaría.
A las señas que tú dieras,   tú eres hermana mía.
—No llores, la mi hermana,   la mi hermana querida.
Si al rey tú perderías,   yo a duques te daría.
25 A la nana, a la buba,   ya se trocan las criaturas.
26 La reina se toma la hija   y la esclava el hijo.

The beginning of the above ballad has been arbitrarily taken from another song. Compare the following variant, whose opening verses, which do not exist in the Bosnian tradition, explain and localize the story.

22. Rodolfo Gil, *Romancero judeo-español* (Madrid, 1911), pp. xxxi–xxxiii; Danon, No. 21. [Baruch consistently favors the "*zersingen* theory," which of late has been subject to increasingly severe criticism. See G. Di Stefano, *Sincronia e diacronia nel Romanzero* (Pisa, 1967), pp. 129–131; id., "Marginalia sul Romanzero," reprinted from *Miscellanea di Studi Ispanici* (Pisa, 1968), pp. 139–178: 154–155; and our review of C. Colin Smith, *Spanish Ballads* (Oxford, 1964), *HR*, XXXVII (1969), 407–412: pp. 408–409.]

La reina Xarifa mora   la que mora en la Almería,
dice que tiene deseos   de una cristiana cautiva.
Los moros como lo oyeran   de repente se partían
de ellos parten para Francia   de ellos para la Almería.
Encuentran al conde Flores   que a la condesa traía....

Next, the queen's Moors capture the countess and kill the count.
Queen and slave give birth on the same day. The Queen recognizes
the slave as her sister when the latter sings a lullaby to her baby:

— ¡ Ay, mi hija de mi alma,   ay mi hija de mi vida!
si nacieras en mis tierras,   grandes señales harías,
te nombraras Blanca flor,   nombre de una hermana mía,
que la cautivaron moros   día de Pascua florida.

The ending, as we can see, is in complete harmony with the beginning. In Bosnia, as I have already mentioned, all traces of local
points of reference are lost; the city of *Almería* is simply replaced
by the word *alegría*, which has the same number of syllables, and
the verse, "si nacieras en mis tierras," is supplanted by "non nacida
de mi tripa."
The following ballad, which tells how a mother recognizes her son
(whom she had cursed because he left his young wife), is well known
among the Jews of Morocco and throughout the entire East. I believe
that this ballad is unknown to Spanish oral and written literature:

[12. *La vuelta del hijo maldecido* (MP 124)]

—¿De qué lloras, Blanca Niña?   ¿De qué lloras, Blanca Flor?
O lloras del mal preñado   o lloras del nuevo amor.
—Lloro por vos, caballero,   que vos vais y me dejáis.
Me dejáis niña muchacha,   a la flor de mi gozar.
5 Ya que vos vais, caballero,   dejadme donde gastar.
Tres hijicos chicos tengo,   lloran y demandan pan.
Encajó su mano al pecho,   cien doblones le fue a dar.
—Esto que me dais, caballero,   no me basta ni para pan.
—Si esto no vos abasta,   ya tenéis de onde gastar.
10 Venderéis campos y viñas,   media parte de ciudad.
—Si ya vos vais, caballero,   decidme cuándo tornáis.
—Si a los ocho no torno,   a los nueve vos casáis.
Y tomáis un mancebico,   que sea mi par igual.
Todos los vestidos míos,   que le vayan al compás.
15 Esto que sintió su madre,   maldición le fue a echar:
—Todas las naves del mundo   vayan y tornen en paz.

Sólo la nave de mi hijo   vaya y no torne más.
Pasó tiempo y vino tiempo,   una barca vino a pasar.
—Así vivas, caballero,   así Dios vos deje gozar,
20 ¿ si visteis al mi hijo,   al mi hijo coronal?
—Bien lo vide, bien lo conozco,   él está echado en un arenal.
La piedra tiene por cabezera,   por cubierta un arenal.
De cada uno de sus granos   entra y sale un gavilán.
Esto que sintió su madre,   a la mar se fue a echar.
25 —No vos echéis, la mi madre,   yo soy vuestro hijo coronal.

The beginning is simply grafted on. This is apparent also in the assonance, which, after the second verse, changes from -ó to -á. It is typical of the traditional diction of this kind of popular poetry to use similar phrases in similar situations. This *romance* is also typical in that it faithfully renders the stylistic elements of Jewish [*read* Spanish?] ballads. In Menéndez Pidal's *Flor nueva de romances viejos*, I found a *romance* (*La condesita*) in which the husband goes to war and leaves his young wife, who, at the moment of their parting, asks him: "¿Cuántos días, cuántos meses / piensas estar por allá?" He answers: "Deja los meses, condesa, / por años debes contar; // si a los tres años no vuelvo, / viuda te puedes llamar."[23] I do not insist, of course, that this *romance* and the Bosnian one have anything in common as far as their stories are concerned.

We will not pass over the following novelesque ballad, which is found only in Bosnia:

[13. *El encuentro del padre* (MP 125)]

Caminí por altas torres,   naveguí por las fortunas,
onde no cantaba gallo,   ni menos canta gallina,
onde bramaban leones,   la leona respondía:
—¿ Qué buscas, hijo del hombre,   qué buscas por estas viñas?
5 —Busco yo al rey mi padre,   la corona que él tenía.
—Una vez que tú lo buscas,   ¿ qué señas por él darías?
—Años tenía sesenta,   la barba blanca tenía.
—A las señas que vos daríais,   el rey turco lo mataría.
Esto que sintió su hijo,   grande lloro lloraría.
10 Arrasgóse los sus paños   de sayo hasta camiza.

23. *Flor*, pp. 251–256. [Actually the two ballads are, at least in part, genetically related. See our commentary in Yoná, No. 23.]

Together with these *romances* on miscellaneous themes, we could also include the following one, which is well known both in Bosnia and in the other Jewish centers, as well as in Spain.[24] Its story is undoubtedly one of the most beautiful. It concerns the motif of the woman-warrior. Our version is, however, somewhat truncated. The girl's heroic deeds are only hinted at and her return home is not even mentioned:

[14. *La doncella guerrera* (MP 121)]

Caballeros van y vienen   por la ciudad de Aragón:
todo el que hijo varón tiene   a la guerra lo envió.
Por ahí pasó un buen viejo,   un buen viejo doblado en dos,
bendiciendo el pan y el vino   y al Dio que se lo dio,
5 maldiciendo la su esposa   que siete hijas le parió,
.... sin ningún hijo varón.
Saltó la más chica y dijo,   la que en buen mazal nació:
—No maldiga, el mi padre,   no maldiga, el mi señor.
Déme armas y caballo,   a la guerra me voy yo.
10 —No hables, la mi hija,   no hables tal deshonor.
Tu hermosa pechadura   no demostra de varón.
—Mi pechadura, el mi padre,   con el paltó la tapo yo.
—Tu hermosa trenzadura   no demostra de varón.
—Mi trenzadura, el mi padre,   con el chapeo la tapo yo.
15 —Tus hermosos coloricos   no demostran de varón.
—Mis colores, el mi padre,   por el aire y el sol las perdo yo.
Tomó armas y caballo   y un vestido de varón.
Tomó armas y caballo   y a la guerra ya partió.
Mesageros van y vienen   que media guerra ya ganó.
20 Guerreando y peleando,   el chapeo le cayó.
—¿Qué vos conte, la mi madre,   lo que hoy me acapitó?
22 Un mancebo vino a la guerra,   hija es y varón no.

Just to show you its beauty, we will quote the following portion of a more complete variant, published by Menéndez Pidal,[25] in which the girl's return home is described:

—¡Corre, corre, hijo del rey,   que no me habrás de alcanzar
hasta en casa de mi padre,   si quieres irme a buscar!
Campanitas de mi iglesia,   ya os oigo repicar;

24. Menéndez Pidal asserts that he has about one hundred variants [*Flor*, p. 244.]
25. *Flor*, p. 243.

puentecito, puentecito,   del río de mi lugar,
una vez te pasé virgen,   virgen te vuelvo a pasar.
Abra las puertas mi padre,   ábralas de par en par.
Madre, sáqueme la rueca,   que traigo ganas de hilar,
que las armas y el caballo   bien los supe manejar.
Tras ella el hijo del rey   a la puerta fue a llamar.

In the Bosnian variant, this passage could also have been omitted because the ballad was a bit too long and perhaps both the singer and his audience were impatient to hear its ending.

The *romance* concerning a girl's vengeance is also very well known in Bosnia. It is very old and is also current in Spain.[26] Its opening section, forgotten in the Spanish versions, is preserved in Morocco. This part is also lacking in Bosnia. It has been compensated for by the addition of several introductory verses, which, by their form, remind us of the beginning of folktales that circulate among the Sephardic Jews. This introductory part is also missing from Abraham Danon's Jewish variant.[27] All the same, the content is harmonious and the dialog is lively and beautiful:

[15. *Rico Franco* (MP 85)]

El buen rey tenía una hija,   una hija muy jarif.
No la daba el su padre   ni por oro, ni por haber,
sino quien la ganaría   en el juego de ajedrez.
Se asentó madre y padre   y sus hermanicos tres.
5 Juega el uno, juega el otro,   no hacen más que perder.
Jugó el morico franco,   la ganó en primera vez
y sigún la ganaría   luego la fue a ver.
Topó la niña llorando   lágrimas dos a tres.
—¿De qué lloras, Blanca Niña,   de qué lloras tú, mi bien?
10 Si lloras por vuestro padre,   carcelero mío es.
Si lloras por vuestra madre,   guisandera mía es.
Si lloras por tus hermanos,   ya los matí a todos tres.
Al más chiquitico de ellos   le di muerte de cruel.
Le cortí cuerpo y mano   y lo hize un finel.
15 —No lloro por padre y madre,   ni por hermanicos tres.
Lloro yo por mi ventura,   que non sé yo cuála es.
—Vuestra ventura está segura;   al lado la tenéis.
—Una vez que sois mi ventura,   asentemos a comer.
En medio de la comida,   le arogó un placer;

26. MP, p. 161.
27. Danon, No. 11.

20 que le diera el cuchillico,　el cuchillico sólo por ver.
　Él se lo dio al derecho;　ella lo tomó al través.
　Asigún lo tomaría,　se lo enfincó por el bel:
23 —Aquí me vengo en madre y padre　y (mis) hermanicos tres.

The incest motif was elaborated in two different ballads in the Judeo-Spanish *Romancero*. The heroine of one of them is *Silvana*; the other is *Delgadilla*. Menéndez Pidal included both in his work on Hispano-Jewish ballads.[28] Abraham Danon published the second.[29] In Bosnia, moreover, Mrs. Laura Papo recorded one such *romance*, sung to her by Flora Abinun in 1917. The heroine is Silvana and the first verse is the same as that of another version concerning this protagonist, which Menéndez Pidal received from Tangier. The Bosnian variant seems somewhat truncated: the beginning and the section just before the end are altogether undeveloped. Of the second theme (*Delgadilla*), Menéndez Pidal states that it is "undoubtedly the most widely-known *romance* in Spain and America":

[16. *Silvana* (MP 98)]

　Pasear se ía Silvana　por el vergel que él tenía.
　—Si te place, hija Silvana,　si te place de ser esta noche mía.
　—Bien me place, el rey mi padre,　me place i me es cortesía.
　Grito da la hija Silvana,　que el cielo aboracaba.
5 Oyó la reina su madre,　de altas torres ahí arriba:
　—¿Qué es esto, hija Silvana,　qué es esto, la hija mía?
　—Vergüenza del rey mi padre,　vergüenza que yo tenía.
　—No llores, hija Silvana,　no llores, la hija mía.
　Troquemos los vestidos　de sayo asta camisa.
10 Ya pasó de la media noche　....................
11 —No es ésta la hija Silvana,　no es ésta la hija mía.

Beside *Arboleda* and *Andarleto*, the best known ballad in Bosnia is *El chuflete*. Here the magic power of the trumpet is described. The motif is known to other literatures as well. The ballad is unknown in Spain, nor does Abraham Danon record it.[30] Menéndez Pidal had received it from Salonika and from Spanish Jews living in Vienna:

28. MP, p. 166.
29. Danon, No. 14.
30. Menéndez Pidal, "Poesía popular y poesía tradicional," p. 30, *n.* 1. [Concerning the exact nature of the *chuflete* 'flute' or 'whistle', which Baruch translates here as 'trumpet,' see Yoná, No. 27, *nn.* 7–9.]

[17. *El chuflete* (MP 142)]

Salir quere el mes de marzo, entrar quere el mes de abril,
cuando el trigo está en grano y las flores por abrir.
Entonces el rey de Alemania a Francia se quiso ir.
Con sí trujo gente mucha, caballeros más de mil.
5 Con sí trujo un chuflete de las ferias de París.
Lo dio el rey de boca en boca, ninguno lo supo sonergir.
—¡ Que mal haya tal chuflete, los doblones que por él di!
Lo tomó el rey en boca y lo supo sonergir.
Todas las naves del mundo, a seco las hizo venir.
10 La parida que está pariendo, sin dolores la hizo parir.
La criatura que está llorando, sin teta la hizo dormir.
La novia que a su novio ama, a su lado la hizo venir.
13 —¡ Que bien haya tal chuflete, que tantos doblones por él di!

We will now quote yet another example of typical balladic diction.
The magic power of song is often treated in the Spanish *Romancero*. The
following instances from ballads in Menéndez Pidal's above-mentioned
Flor nueva de romances viejos prove that our Jewish text follows the
line of the Spanish tradition. Conde Niño gives water to his horse and,
while the horse is drinking, he sings a song, with the following results:

> todas las aves del cielo se paraban a escuchar,
> caminante que camina olvida su caminar,
> navegante que navega la nave vuelve hacia allá.[31]

In another ballad (*El infante Arnaldos*), a boatman sings a song:

> que la mar ponía en calma, los vientos hace amainar;
> los peces que andan al hondo, arriba los hace andar;
> las aves que van volando, al mástil vienen posar.[32]

On the basis of what we have said, our readers may have formed a
certain idea about the themes of the *romances* and their character
and form. Using available bibliography, we have also tried to present
data concerning the connections of the Bosnian ballad tradition with
that of Spain, on one hand, and with that of other Hispano-Jewish
centers, on the other. There are, however, a certain number of poems,
mostly on lyric subjects, whose divergence from the *romances* is immediately apparent. These songs often lack epico-narrative elements
and are all written in shorter lines. Among such poems, the following
song is well known in Bosnia:

31. [*Flor*, p. 157.]
32. [*Flor*, p. 245.]

[18. *Morena me llaman*]

Morena me llaman,   yo blanca nací.
De pasear, galana,   mi color perdí.
Morena me llama   el hijo del rey.
Si otra vez me llama,   con él me iré.
. . . .

Or this one, which was sung for me by a female resident of Skoplje:

[19. *El sueño profético* (MP 68)]

La reina de Francia   tres hijas tenía.
La una labraba,   la otra cosía.
La más chiquitica   bastidor tenía.
. . . .
. . . .

Some, again, have the *romance* verse, but are strophic in form. Here is one of them, sung for me by another Skoplje girl. Its theme is the love between a girl and an unfaithful young man. It has a certain beauty. This is the last stanza:

[20. *Morenico sos*]

Morenico sos, querido;
para mí una kondžá.
Muchas niñas engañates;
lo mío salió verdad.

All these characteristics are, however, merely of a formal nature. The fact that neither their spirit nor their content has any connection with the written or oral tradition of the unusually rich treasury of the Spanish *Romancero* shows that these songs are not *romances* in the strict literary-historical sense. The same may be said of those many poems, created for various occasions, which are popular among the Bosnian Jews. Such are those sung at weddings, circumcisions, the leave-taking of pilgrims going to Jerusalem, etc. All of them are important as cultural-historical documents, but they have nothing to do with the Spanish tradition. For this reason, we will not be concerned with them here.

Finally, we must again stress that this article does not pretend to be a complete monograph. To write such a work, one would have to engage in longer and more detailed research based upon an acquaintance with the interpreters of the *romance* themselves. Not having done this rather extensive preliminary work, I have used, as already mentioned, the materials that I myself own, as well as those provided for me by Mrs. Laura Papo. Once more I thank her for her kind cooperation and assistance.

Three Sephardic Ballads

(Sung in 1932 at the concert of the Jewish choral society "Lyre"
in Sarajevo)

Harmonized by B. Jungić

Tri sefardske romanse*

harmonizovao: B.Jungić

Quien madre no tiene...

Quien madre no tie-ne mucho la de:-

se - a yo que la te - ní - a

en tie - rra a - je - na

* Pjevane god. 1932 na koncertu Jevr. pjevačkog društva
. Lira' u Sarajevu

Arboleda

290

En la mar hay una torre...

C.

"BALLADS OF THE BOSNIAN SEPHARDIM"

Published in the Newspaper *Jevrejski Glas* (1939)

Sometime during 1939 the editors of the Sephardic newspaper *Jevrejski Glas* ("The Jewish Voice") of Sarajevo initiated a column which was to stimulate the interest of a number of their readers. The purpose of this editorial innovation is described in the following sensitive essay, which accompanied the first in a series of traditional ballads to be collected and edited in subsequent months:

Life passes by. All things exist only in a given time and place. Everything that only yesterday seemed inseparable from our everyday life, a part of our very selves, today is being more or less forgotten and replaced by new things. We may agree or disagree with this; we may look forward to the arrival of the new or grieve over the disappearance of the old. It makes little difference; the fact remains. There are things, however, which we must try to save from oblivion, because they are a part of our milieu, a part of a people's soul, of a community—its tradition, its sorrow, its joy, and its dreams—a part of all that constitutes the reality of a given moment. Song was always the most direct reflection of that reality. The Bosnian Sephardic Jews have their own song, their own so-called Spanish *romansa*. Indeed, it is characterized by many traces of Spanish feudalism; but there are still many songs which are quite immediate; they express the cares of everyday life, of the common man, his sorrow and his joy, his love and his disillusionment. Several attempts have been made to write about the ballad more seriously and in greater depth, to find its sources and origins, but no one has ever tried to collect as many versions as possible of these songs which are disappearing under the impact of modernizing pressures. The editors of the *Jevrejski Glas* decided to start a movement for collecting all songs in Spanish which are still heard among the Sephardic Jews in our country. We therefore ask all our readers and friends to copy down every song in Spanish which they hear in their homes, among their relatives, or in the circle of their friends. We will always give the name of the person who recorded the song and where it was heard. It would be of particular interest to know of several versions of the same song and, for this reason, we ask our friends not to be confused if they find a certain song published in slightly different form from the version which they know. Let them send us their own versions. In each issue we will publish one song. We hope that this effort of ours will one day serve to provide material for a more detailed study and analysis of this interesting branch of the Spanish ballad in general. If we succeed in this, our goal will have been attained.[1]

1. The column, which accompanies ballad No. 16, ends with the following statement: "As can be seen from this first published song, we will print them in the form in which they are preserved; that is, as they were pronounced,

There is something deeply moving about the gentleness and respect toward their informants, as well as in the great seriousness—a combination of antiquarianism, nostalgia, and intense cultural pride—with which the editors of the *Jevrejski Glas* approach their self-imposed task of perpetuating the ancient folk poetry of the Sarajevo community. The brief comments which they often print following the ballads contributed by their readers bespeak a painstaking concern for detail, an interest in close textual comparison (No. 13B), and attention to the importance of reconstructing fragmentary texts (No. 15). In several cases, the editors even go so far as to print minute variant readings and emendations to ballads published in earlier issues (see Nos. 10, 16, 21). Their comments sometimes take the form of an insistent plea to their readers, as in a note to text No. 10, where they follow up their initial call for ballads:

> This week we publish a second *romansa* in this new column of our newspaper. The cordial acceptance with which this announcement was received in large circles of our readers is the best proof of how alive and cherished the ballad still is among all of us. We will try to publish all those songs which can be heard and are sung among us, but again we ask all of our readers and friends to write down everything they hear from their mothers and from elderly women.

Again, following text 19, they announce:

> This week we received, from various friends, several ballads which we will print at a later date. We expect that our other friends will also remember to write down those songs which are still heard in their family circles and which have not yet been printed by us.

A sense of enthusiasm and achievement permeates a note adjoining text 7:

> It has now been seven months since we started publishing ballads. The great interest with which our enterprise has been greeted has lived up to our expectations. Again we ask all our readers to send us every *romansa* which they may hear around them.

---

phonetically. A linguist who may put this material in order at some later date will have no difficulty in converting it into the original Spanish orthography and transcription. For our readers, who generally read phonetic spelling with less difficulty, our way of writing will be easier and more understandable." Lest phonological nuances be lost, we have not accepted the editors' suggestion but have left intact their original—and quite satisfactory—Serbo-Croatian orthography.

Romanse bosan-
skih Sefarada

KEN MADRE NO TIENE

Ken madre no tiene
mučo la dizeja,
eja ke la tenia
por tieras aženas.

Sola se vistia
sola se kalsava,
sola i asolada
el parto le tomava.

»Alivanteš mi rej
alivanteš mi konte,
a la vuestra madre
a jamar la fueraš«.

Si alevanto el rej .
si alevanto el konte,
a puertas de su ma'
aji li amanisiria.

»Ken se este pero
ken se este konte,

ke a talas oras
a mi puerta bate«.

»No so ningun pero
ni menos so konte,
si no so su ižo
ke a jamar la vengo,
ke a la luz del dia
el parto li tomava«.

Esto ke sentio su madre
si fue a la salera
tomo sal de la salera
si fue a ensembrar a la guerta.

»Kuando esta sal eča flores
mi nuera tomi las dolores,
kuando eča ožas,
mi nuera este entre las ničozas'·

Parto en lejas tierras (No. 9, vv. 1–17)
as printed in the *Jevrejski Glas*

Indeed, the editors had good reason to be proud both of their own efforts and of their readers' response. Ballad scholars, both Hispanic and Pan-European, owe a dept of gratitude to the unknown editors of *Jevrejski Glas*, who on the eve of the unsuspected holocaust which was to engulf their community, had the foresight to perpetuate in printed form the ephemeral but precious folk poetry of their forefathers.

The *Jevrejski Glas* ballads have come to us in the form of loose, undated clippings bearing no identification of the newspaper's editors or of the pages or issues in which the various ballads were published.[2] Apparently No. 16 was the first text in the series, followed by No. 10; No. 19 was third (cf. the editorial notes to these ballads). No. 7 was probably one of the last to be printed. The column devoted to the ballads is usually entitled *Romanse bosanskih Sefarada*, each ballad's first hemistich or its first few words being generally represented as its title. An exception is No. 5, which is given the title *Merkedeš senjora* (= v. 5). The name of the person contributing the ballad is usually, but not always, mentioned after the text.[3] Two *romances* are provided with geographic indications (No. 8, from Sarajevo, and No. 13B, from Travnik). One text is dated November 1939 (No. 13B). In the original printing, each hemistich appears as a separate verse, every four hemistichs usually being grouped as a quatrain. The ballads are written in Serbo-Croatian orthography. Some of the peculiarities of this system are worth noting: $đ = j$ in Eng. *Jim*; $dž = j$ in Eng. *John*; $j = y$ in Eng. *you*; $ć$ (= *ch* in Eng. *cheese*) alternates with $č$ (= *ch* in Eng. *church*) in the *Jevrejski Glas'* transcription; $c = ts$. We have supplied accents according to academic norms and have freely modified capitalization, punctuation, and word division. Verse numbers have been supplied. Where possible, the ballads have been identified, numbered, and arranged in the order in which corresponding text-types occur in Menéndez Pidal's "Catálogo." *Romansa*, the Serbo-Croatian (and Judeo-Spanish) term used in the newspaper, is either rendered as "ballad" or simply left untranslated.

2. The clippings sent to us by Rabbi Gaon include nine lyric songs which we do not publish at this time. Did Kalmi Baruch, who was a contributor to the *Jevrejski Glas* (see *Spomenica*, p. 290), help motivate the newspaper's ballad harvest? Perhaps some of *our* readers may be able to inform us of the identity of the *Jevrejski Glas'* editors.

3. The following contributors are identified: Aron Abinun (1, 6, 8, 19); V. Altarac (17); Moric Atijas (1); Rifka, widow of H. Avram Atijas (18); J. Katan (10, 16); Rabbi Mordehaj Z. Konforte (20); Moric Konforte (5); Laura Papo ("Bohoreta") (10, var.); Sara (or Saru), [wife of] Moše Papo (2, 4, 12, 14). The initials "St. P." appear after ballad No. 3. Nos. 7, 9, 11, 13A–B, 15, and 21 are anonymous.

1. *Melisenda insomne* (MP 28)
+ *Choza del desesperado* (MP 140)

—¡Noćes, noćes, buenas noćes,   noćes son de namorar,
  ¡ah! noćes son de namorar!

Esta noće, la mi madre,   no la puedo somportar,
  ¡ah! no la puedo somportar,

dando bueltas por la kama   komo el peše en la mar,
  ¡ah! komo el peše en la ma[r].

—Trez ižikas čikas tengo,   todas tres a una edad,
  ¡ah! todas tres a una edad.

5 Saltó la primera i dišo: —Gozemos la mosidad,
  ¡ah! gozemos la mosidad.

Amanjana espozamos,   no aj más kvando gozar,
  ¡ah! no aj más kvando gozar.

Saltó la sigunda i dišu: —Gozemos la novjedad,
  ¡ah! gozemos la novjedad.

Amanjana mos kazamos,   no aj más kvando gozar,
  ¡ah! no aj más kvando gozar.

Saltó la trisera i dišu: —Madre, ¿ kómo la vo dešar,
  ¡ah! madre, kómo la vo dešar ?

10 Jirme kero, la me madre,   por los kampos kvantos son,
  ¡ah! por los kampos kvantos son.

Jervizikas de el kampo   por pan me las komeré,
  ¡ah! por pan me las komeré.

Lágrimas de los mis ožos   por agva me las biviré,
  ¡ah! por agva me las biviré.

I en medjo de el kampo,   kastijo me fragvaré,
  ¡ah! kastijo me fragvaré.

Todo ke pur ají pasa,   ariva jo lo jamaré,
  ¡ah! ariva jo lo jamaré.

15 El ke konte sus males;   jo los míos kontaré,
  ¡ah! jo los míos kontaré.

Si los sujos son más grandes,   kon pansensja jo los jevaré,
  ¡ah! kon pansensja jo los jevaré.

17 Si los mívos son más grandes,   del kastijo abašo me ečaré,
  ¡ah! del kastijo me ečaré.

([Moric] Atijas and Aron Abinun)

Note by the editors of *Jevrejski Glas*: "We received this ballad from two of our friends, Mr. Atijas and Mr. Aron Abinun. There were no essential differences between their variant texts except in the order of some of the strophes. Besides this ballad, we received from these gentlemen several more *romansas*, which we will eventually publish."

2. *Hero y Leandro* (MP 41)

Trez ermanikas eran,   trez ermanikas son.
Doz estavan kazadas,   la čika a la perdisjón.
   ¡Ah, morenika,
   morenika i savrozika
   i su kara di flor!
Su padre, de vringuensa,   a la Francia la mandó.
   ¡Ah, morenika,
   morenika i savrozika
   i su kara di flor!
In medjo de mares,   kastiljo le fraguó,
5 kon pjedras menudas   i kal al deredor,
   ¡Ah, morenika,
   morenika i savrozika
   i su kara di flor!
ventanas a el mares,   ke no entre varón.
   ¡Ah, morenika,
   morenika i savrozika
   i su kara di flor.
Varón ke lo supo,   a nadar se ečó,
   ¡Ah, morenika,
   morenika i savrozika
   i su kara di flor!
nadando i navigando,   jamando la Blanka[f]lor.
   ¡Ah, morenika,
   morenika i savrozika
   i su kara di flor!
Morena dormjendo,   la boz li konesjó.
   ¡Ah, morenika,
   morenika i savrozika
   i su kara di flor!
10 Ečó sus trensados,   ariva lo asuvjó.
   ¡Ah, morenika,
   morenika i savrozika
   i su kara di flor!

Avrijóle la kaša　i de modar le djo.
　¡Ah, morenika,
　morenika i savrozika
　i su kara di flor!

Metjóle la meza;　a senar le djo.
　¡Ah, morenika,
　morenika i savrozika
　i su kara di flor!

13 Ízole la kama;　a dormir lo ečó.
　¡Ah, morenika,
　morenika i savrozika
　i su kara di flor!

(Sara, [wife of] Moše Papo)

8b　*Letter is damaged or worn away.*

3. *Virgilios* (MP 46)

Pasióse Doverdjeli　por los palasios del re,
por jamar una donzelja,　suvrina del re.
Esto el re ke supo,　no le hue a plazer.
I jamó a su đente:　—Akí, đente del re.
5 Tomaréš a Doverdjeli,　al karsel lo meteréš
i las javes del karseljo　a mí me las trajeréš.
Siete anjos en karseljo,　ninguno viene a él ver.
Su madre, la disdiča,　kada día lo va a ver.
Estando el re a la ventana,　vido pasar una mužer,
10 ke vestida va de preto　de kavesa fin los pies.
Demandó el re a su đente:　—¿ Kén es esta mužer,
ke de preto va vestida　de kavesa fin los pies?
—Madre es de Doverdjeli,　ke al karsel lo tenéš.
Demandó el re de su đente　las javes del karsel,
15 por ver a Doverdjeli,　ke en karseljo lo tiene él.
—Siete anjos estó en karseljo,　en el karsel del re.
Si al buen re le plaze,　estaré asta los dies.
Preguntó el re a su đente:　—Venid akí, đente del re.
Tomaréš a Doverdjeli,　al banjo lo jevaréš.
20 Dalde los kavajos,　los ke enbeneja el re.
21 Dalde a la donse[lj]a,　la ke él la jama Sadé.

(St. P.)

2a　por jamar: *read* por amar.
8a　disdiča: *read* disdičada.
21a　*Letters damaged or worn away.*

4. *Hermanas reina y cautiva* (MP 48)

—Morikos, los mis morikos,   los ke para Francia ijan,
trajgádešme una esklava,   una esklava kativa.
Ke no seja de baša đente,   ni menos de en vía en vía,
sino de dukes i de kontes,   de una vanda muj valida.
5 Ja se parten los morikos,   ja se parten, ja se ijan.
Ja li traen la esklava,   la esklava kativa.
Ke no era de baša đente,   ni menos de vía en vía,
sino de dukes i de kontes,   de una vanda muj valida.
Pasan días, vienen días: . . . .
10 Ja enprenja la rena   i la esklava en un día.
Ja les toman las dolores   a todas dos en un día.
Ja mandan por las komadres,   las komadres más validas.
La rena parió una iža   i la esklava un ižo.
Las komadres hueron agudas,   trokan a las kreaturas:
15 A la rena le dan el ižo,   a la esklava la iža.
La rena se eča en la kamareta   i la esklava en la kuzina.
La rena kome gajinas,   la esklava tarajinas.
La rena kome pičones,   la esklava makarones.
Pasan días, vienen días,   ja los ečan a la kama.
20 Kantava la esklava,   kantava a su kreatura:
—A la nana i a la buba,   se durma esta kreatura.
Kreada de los mis pečos,   no nasida de mis tripas.
Si tú eras mi kreatura   ¿ké nombre jo te metía?
Metiérate Flor-de-las-flores,   nombre de una ermana mía.
25 Kon estas palavras diziendo,   el buen rej ke ja venía.
—Así bivas, la esklava,   torna kanta esta kantiga.
27 Por la kavesa de el buen rej,   nada to te aré.

(Saru, [wife of] Moše Papo)

9b   *We supply dots indicating a missing hemistich.*
27b   nada to te aré 'nada jo te aré' (?)

5. *Don Bueso y su hermana* (MP 49)

—Alivantéme, madre, un día de manjanika.
Me hue de lavar la kara onde el sol salía.

Salieron tres moros, me katevarían.
A otro renado a mí me jevarían.

5 —Merkedeš, seniora, a esta linda esklava,
ke en todo vuestro renado no aj más galana.

Tomedeš, seniora, tomedeš esta kativa,
ke en todo vuestro renado no aj más valida.

—¿ Para ké jo kero a esta esklava luzía ?
10 El rej es mansevo, se la tomará por amiga.

—Kítale, seniora, el bever del vino.
Perderá su kolor i kovrará suspiro.

Kítale, seniora, el dormir del klaro.
Perderá su kolor i kovrará dezmajo.

15 Kuanto máz le kita el bever del vino,
máz se le resiende su kolor valido.

Kuanto más le kita el dormir del klaro,
máz se le resiende su kolor galana.

—Mándala, seniora, a lavar al río,
20 ke lave los panjos, los panjos i los linos.

Mándala de manjana a lavar al río.
Perderá kolores, kovrará suspiros.

—¡O pies en la agua, en la agua jelada!
Por ají pasó un kavajero ke de la gera venía.

25 —¡Oh, ké pačás blankas en agua jelada!
I dízimi tú, njinja, si me kereš por kompanjo.

—Bien me plaze, kavaljero, bien me plaze por mi vida.
Los panjos del río, no sé ké los aría.

—Los vestidos de oro, ensima del mi kavajo,
30 los de lana i seda, al río dešaldos.

Kaminando kampos, kampos i vinjas:
—¡Aj kampos, aj kampos, kampos de Oliva!

Kuandro el rej mi padre ensembró la oliva,
la rena mi madre al kampo mi kitaría.
35 Entonses los moros me katevarían.

¡Aj kampos, aj kampos, kampos de Granada!
Kuandro el rej mi padre ensembró la granada,
enstonses los moros a mí me katevarían.

—A las senjas ke me darías,   tú eras ermana mía.
40 Ja se bezan, ja se abrasan   el mansevo i la njinja.
—Avradeš, mi madre,   puertas del palasjo.
Ke en lugar de nuera,   la iža vos trajgo.
—Si es la mi nuera,   prontos mis siljeros.
Si es la mi iža,   prontos los mis pečos.
45 Ja si bezan, ja si abrasan,   la madre i la iža.

(Moric Konforte)

13b, 17b   el dormir del klaro (*meaning?*). *In parallelistic couplets* klaro *is a synonym for* vino. *The verses' original reading was doubtless* el bever del klaro. *What new meaning the singer may have attributed to the altered verse remains problematic.*
33a, 37a   Kuandro: *Read* Kuando?

Note by the editors of *Jevrejski Glas*: "We publish this ballad from the collection brought together by Mr. Moric Konforte."

6. *Conde Olinos* (MP 55)

—Iža mía, mi kerida,   ven tú una noće a la mi udá.
Sentirás kantar ermozo   a la serena de la mar.
—Serena de mar, me madre,   ni kantó ni va kantar,
sino es un manseviko   ke a mí me kere alkansar.
5 Kantará día i noći,   a mí no mi alkansará.
Esto ke sentjó su madre,   presto lo mandó a matar.
I dispués ke lo matan,   ke lo ečen a kemar
i akea sinizika,   ke la ečen a la mar.
Ke de ají sali la perla,   perla fina i buen koral.
10 Esto ke sentió la iža,   presto lo korjó a salvar.
Eja se izo una palomba,   él se izo un gavelán.
Volan, volan, ¿ónde apodzan?   A los palasios del pašá.
Ají si topó un espino   ke no los dešava gozar.
Volan, volan, ¿ónde apodzan?   A los konakes del vezir.
15 Ají si topó un espino   ke no los deša bevir.

(Aron Abinun)

7. *La vuelta del marido* (*i*) (MP 58)

Arvoleda, arvoleda,   arvoleda tan đentil,
en la rama de más ariva   aj una bolisa d'Amadí,
penjándose sus kavejos   kon un penje de marfil;
la raíz tiene de oro,   la cimenta de marfil.
5 Por ají pasó un kavajero,   kavajero tan đentil:
  —¿ Ké buškas, la mi bolisa?   ¿ Ké buškas vos por akí? [. . . .]
  —¿ Kuánto davaš, la mi bo[lisa],   ke vos lo traigan akí?
  —Dava jo los tres mis ka[mpos]   ke me kedaron de Amadí.
El uno arava trigo   i el otro zeđefil;
10 el más čikitiko de ejos,   trigo blanko para Amadí.
  —¿ Más ké davaš, la mi bolis[a],   ke vos lo traigan akí?
  —Dava jo mis tres molinos   ke kedaron de Amadí.
El uno molía klavo   i el otro zenđefil;
el más čikitiko de ejos,   arina blanka para Amadí.
15   —¿ Más ké davaš, la mi bolisa,   ke vos lo traigan akí?
  —Dava jo las tres mis ižas   ke me kedaron de Amadí.
La una para la meza,   la otra para servir,
la más čikitika de ejas   para olgar i para dormir.
  —¿ Davos a vos, la mi bolisa,   ke vos lo traigan akí?
20   —Mal anjo tal kavajero   ke tal me kižo dezir.
  —¿ Ké senjal daš, la mi bolisa,   ke vos lo traigan akí?
  —Bašo la teta siarda   tiene un ben maví.
  —No maldigas, la mi bolisa,   jo so vuestro marido Amadí.
Ečadvos vuestro trensado,   me suviré jo par ají.
25 Tomaron mano kon mano,   sa fueron a olgar.

7a, 8a, 11a   *Type is damaged or worn away.*
19a   Davos: *read* Davaš.
25b   sa: *read* se.

8. *La novia abandonada* (MP 67)

Una tarde de las tardes,   jéndomi para minhá,
eskontrí una mučača,   ermoza era en kantidat.
Tante hue su ermozura,   ke me ija jo a dezmajar.
El mansevo vjene en kaza;   el non es kadir de arepozar.
5 —¿ Lu ke es estos, el mi ižo,   ke no sos kadir de arepozar ?
—Una tarde de las tardes,   jéndomi para minhá,
eskontrí una mučača,   ¡ak! ermozura era en kantidad.
Demandísela al padre,   por ver s'es ke me la keri dar.
Me dišo ke no mi la da,   ke no tjene iža de espozar.
10 Demandísela a la madre,   por ver s'es ke me la keri dar.
Me dišo ke non mi la da,   ¡ah! me dišo ko non me la keri dar.
Demandísela al ermano,   por ver s'es ke me la keri dar.
13 Esto ke sintjó el ermano,   kon plomo kurjó a mi dar.

(Aron Abinun, Sarajevo)

3a   Tante: *read* Tanta.
5a   estos: *read* esto.
11b ko: *read* ke.
13b *The verse is obscure:* 'He hastened to strike me with lead.' Or did he fire lead
     bullets ? Cf. No. 16, v. 23b.

9. *Parto en lejas tierras* (MP 68)

Ken madre no tiene   mučo la dizeja.
Eja ke la tenía   por tieras aženas.
Sola se vistía,   sola se kalsava,
sola i asolada   el parto le tomava.
5 —Alivantéš, mi rej,   alivantéš, mi konte,
a la vuestra madre   a jamarla fueraš.
Si alevantó el rej,   si alevantó el konte,
a puertas de su ma[dre],   ají le amanisiría.
—¿ Kén se este pero?   ¿ Kén se este konte,
10 ke a talas oras   a mi puerta bate ?
—No so ningún pero,   ni menos so konte,
sino so su ižo   ke a jamarla vengo,
ke a la Luz-del-día   el parto li tomava.
Esto ke sentió su madre,   si fue a la salera.
15 Tomó sal de la salera,   si fue a ensembrar a la guerta:

—Kuando esta sal eča flores,   mi nuera tomi las dolores.
Kuando eča ožas,   mi nuera esté entre las ničozas.

—Si no mi eráš madre   i mi eráš madrasta,
kon la espada ke tengo   la kavesa vos ketava.

20 Se alevantó el rej,   se alevantó el konde,
a puertas de su kaza   ají le amanisía.

—Paridvos, mi alma,   paridvos, mi vida,
ke la mía madre   en kaza no staría.

—Se la vuestra madre   venir no kería,
25 vajáš onde la mía,   enlugo vos venía.
Si alevantó el rej,   si alevantó el konde,
a puerta de su shuegra   ají le amanesía.

—¿ Kén es este rej ?   ¿ Kén se este konde,
ke a talas oras   en mi puerta batía ?

30 —No so ningún rej,   ni menos so konde,
ke so jo su jerno   ke a jamarla vengo,
ke a la Luz-del-día   el parto le tomaría.

Esto ke sintó su madre,   si fue al gajinero:
—Komo kulaj paren las [gajinas],   ansí para la mi iža.

35 Ja viene la madre   kon las manos jenas.
En una mano jeva   jervas de paridas.
En la otra jeva   masos de kandelas.

En medio del kamino,   sentió una kampanera,
una kampanera   muj amarga i muj afrita.

40 —Así bivaš, kampanero,   ¿ por kén es esta kampanera ?
¿ Por kén es esta kampanera   tan amarga i tan afrita ?

—Por una manseva   ke del partu moriría.
Esto ke sintió su madre,   de la montanja abašo se [ečaría].

—Viréš, mis vizinas,   viréš ké manzía:
45 La madre i la iža,   todas dos en un día.

8a, 34a, 43b   *Type is damaged or worn away.*
9a–b, 28b   se: *read* es.
33a   sintó: *read* sintió.

10. *La malcasada del pastor* (MP 72)

Mi madre era di Brusa,　mi padre d'Aragón.
Si kazaron enđunto,　nasjérami jo.
Por ke era regalada,　čika mi kazó.
Mi djeron por marido　a un riko pastor.
5 Entre la pastoría　non lo aj mižor.
Al mez di kazada,　una preva me aprevó.
A la fin de la media noće,　agva mi demandó.
Agva non avía en kaza,　a la huente me mandó.
La huente era lešos,　el eshuenjo mi kajó.
10 Por ají pasó un kavajero,　trez bezikos mi dio.
—Si el mi marido lo　save,　matada seré jo.
Antez ke él me mate,　mi mataré jo.
13 —Non te mates, mi alma,　ke jo so el tu amor.

(J. Katan)

Note by the editors of *Jevrejski Glas* (appended to No. 19): "Mrs.
Laura Papo ('Bohoreta') asserts that the first verse of our second
romansa really should read: 'Mi madre era di Francia' and not 'di
Brusa.' However, one can hear 'di Brusa' more often than 'di Francia.'
It is the duty of researchers to discover how this change in the names
of these cities, which are actually very far from each other, occurred.
Our duty is, as we said earlier, only to record." This is undoubtedly
the same Laura Papo who informed for Kalmi Baruch six years earlier.
Concerning this prominent member of the Sarajevo community, see
R. Ovadija's article in *Spomenica*, pp. 305 ff.

11. *La mujer engañada* (MP 74)

¡Džam, džam,   farfulí findžán!
Mi lo iči a la kama,   mi se fujó por el džam.
Korí de detrás,   por ver óndi ija.
Lo vide entrar   ondi la blanka njinja.
   I mueva amor.
5 Entrí jo adjentro   por ver lo ke avía.
Vidi mezas prontas   kon beljas komidas.
   I mueva amor.
Entrí máz adjentro   por ver lo ke avía.
Vidi kamas prontas   kon beljas kortinas.
   I mueva amor.
Entrí máz adjentro   por ver lo ke avía.
10 Vide al malfadado   burlando kon la njinja.
   I mueva amor.
Ni ez más galana,   ni ez más valida,
karika enkalada,   sežika entenjida.
   I mueva amor.
Torníme a kaza   triste i amargina.
Mi sarí la puerta   kon sjeti trankinas.
   I mueva amor.
15 A la media noći,   la njinja jorava.
—Dórmite, mi alma,   dórmite, mi vista.
   I mueva amor.
Dórmite, mi alma,   dórmite, mi vista,
ke el tu padre estava   burlando kon la njinja.
   I mueva amor.
Avlando estas palavrikas,   a la puerta batía:
20 —Avrími, mi alma,   avrími, mi vista.
   I mueva amor.
Avrími, mi alma,   avrími, mi vista,
ki vengo kansado   der arode las vinjas.
   I mueva amor.
—No viníš kansado   de arodear las vinjas,
ke veníš kansado   de burlar kon la njinja.
   I mueva amor.
25 Amaniser amanisiría,   onde el haham iría.
26 Sultura le daría,   maz no lu kería.
   I mueva amor.

22b   *Text is corrupt; it should read the same as 23b.*

12. *La adúltera* (ó) (MP 78)

—El buen rej si hue a la gera, a la gera de Anadol.
Vengan moros i lo maten, kazaréme jo kon vos.
En estas palavras diziendo, el buen rej ke ja tornó.
—Ávreme, mi blanka njinja, ávreme, mi ermoza flor.
5 Ke aze luvia menodika, me se moža el kontor.
—Si el kontor era de panjo, de seda vo lo aré jo.
Si el kontor era de seda, de sirma vo lo aré jo.
Ravja le suvió al buen rej, ke la puerta izo en dos.
Topa a la njinja jorando lágrimas a dos i a tres.
10 —¿De ké joras, blanka njinja, de ké joras, mi ermoza flor?
—Joro ke perdí las javes, las javes del koredor.
—Si las javes son de fjero de sirma vo las aré jo.
—Dízemi, mi blanka njinja, dízemi, mi ermoza flor:
¿Di kén es este kavajo, este kavajo ke vejo jo?
15 —Este kavajo, el buen rej, el mi padre se lo mandó,
para ke gane la gera, la gera de Anadol.
—Dízemi, mi blanka njinja, dízemi, mi ermoza flor:
¿Di kén son estas kundurias, estas kundurias ke vejo jo?
—Estas kundurias, el buen rej, el mi padre mi las mandó,
20 para ke sjerva al buen rej de alma i de korasón.
—Dízemi, mi blanka njinja, dízemi, mi ermoza flor:
¿Di kén son estas armadas, estas armadas ke vejo jo?
—Estas armadas, el buen rej, el mi padre se las mandó,
para ke gane la gera, la gera de Anadol.
25 —Dízemi, blanka njinja, dízemi, mi ermoza flor:
¿Kén es éste de la kamareta, de la kamareta ke vejo jo?
—Sjegen ožos ke tal vienen a mirar fin al kantón.
—Ven akí, mi blanka njinja, ven akí, mi ermoza flor.
Verás tú lo ke aré jo, lo ke aré de todos dos.
30 Kortóles pies i manos, muerte dioles de kruel.

(Saru, [wife of] Moše Papo)

13A. *La adúltera* (*á-a*) (MP 80)

—Burđula, la mi Burđula,   ¿ kén bate tan de manjana?
—El mosiko del panadero;   levadura mos demanda.
Levadura mos demanda;   arina no aj en kaza.
—Marido, el mi marido,   alivántisi de manjana.
5 Ke el ganado de la manjana   no lo aj entre la semana.
El marido por la puerta;   el namorado por la ventana.
En medjo de el kamino,   laz javes se olvidó.
Tornó el marido en kaza: —Mužer, ávrima la puerta.
Ke los pjes tengo en la njevi,   la kavesa en la jelada.
10 —¿ Kómo ke te avra, mi alma,   kómo ke te avra, mi bjen?
Al ižo tengo en la alda,   al malfadado en la kama.
¿ Ónde ke te skonda, mi alma?   ¿ Ónde ke te skonda, mi bjen?
A la kaša di la pimjenta: el močačo sarnudava.
—Mužer, la mi mužer,   ¿ kén sarnuda en esta kaša?
15 —El gatiko de la vizina;   ratonikos mos afara.
—Mužer, la mi mužer,   dami las javes de la kaša.
Dami las javes de la kaša,   por ver komo los afara.
—El día de la kolada,   pardí las javes de la kaša.
—Anda ondi la vizina;   ke voz empreste la sujas.
20 —No ozo, el mi marido,   ke'stá [el] vezino en kaza.
Ke el vezino stá en kaza   i después si le aravja.
Tomó la baltá en su mano,   izo la kaša en kvatro pedasos.
—Vizinas, las mis vizinas,   las d'abašo i las d'ariva,
vení, viréš gato kon barva   i mostačikos retorsidos.
25 Ken tjene možer ermoza,   ke la miri bjen gvardar,
26 ki vjene el gato i si la jeva   i él kedará sin nada.

([Sarajevo])

8b   ávrima: *read* ávrime.
19b   la sujas: *read* las sujas.
21a   Ke el: *originally* Ke' el.

The words "Nastaviće se" ('To be continued') follow the text. Obviously this refers to the newspaper's ballad column and not to the ballad itself.

13B. *La adúltera* (*á-a*) (MP 80)

—Burđula, la mi Burđula,   ¿ kén bate tan de manjana?   (1)
—El mosiko de la vezina;   levadura mos demanda.   (2)
—Marido, el mi marido,   alivántisi de manjana.   (4)
Ke el trato de la manjana   es por entera la semana.   (5)
5 El marido por la puerta;   el namorado por la ventana.   (6)
—Mužer, la mi mužer,   ¿ kén sarnuda en esta kaša?   (14)
—El gatiko de la vizina;   ratonikos moz afara.   (15)
Tomí baltá en mi mano,   por ver lu ke aj en la kaša.   (22)
—Vizinas, las mis vizinas,   las d'abašo i las d'ariva,   (23)
10 vení, viréš gatu kon barva,   mostačikos aretorsidos.   (24)
Ken tjene možer ermoza,   ki la miri bjen gvardarla.   (25)
12 Si no, vjene el gato rojo,   si la jeva i él keda sin nada. (26)

(Anonymous, Travnik, November, 1939)

4a   Ke el: *originally* Kel el.

Note by the editors of *Jevrejski Glas*: "We received this well-known ballad from a friend in Travnik. At the same time, we received the same song from a man in Sarajevo, but in another version. This other version [= 13A] differs from the present one both textually and in length. Because of interesting details, we ask our esteemed readers to keep the present issue of our newspaper so that they themselves can compare this version with the one which we will publish in the next issue."

14. *El raptor pordiosero* (MP 92)

—Siete anjos andava   por la njinja blanka:
no me la dešavan ver   ni por oro, ni por plata.
Me ize maromero,   maromero de la ruina.
Le hue a la puerta,   la almoza le pedíja.
5 —Alevántate, me iža,   la máz čikitika,
a dalde la almoza,   ke de vos la pedíja.
—Nunka vide, madre,   este maromero,
dándole la almoza,   me apretó el dedo.
—Sjego stó, senjora,   ke no vejo gota,
10 a palpos i a palpones   tomí la almoza.
Amostra, mi senjora,   puertas de kastijo.
Tomóla por la mano,   manija de oro en braso.

El ke la vido sola,   sola por el kampo,
bezóla i abrasóla,   ečóla en su kavajo.

15 El ke la vido sola,   sola por las vinjas,
bezóla i abrasóla,   ečóla en su sija.

—De dukes i kontes   jo hue demandada;
de un maromero   jo hue enganjada.

—I jo so el duke   i jo so el konte,
20 ižo so del re de Francia,   re de India.

—Viteš, mis vizinas,   viteš mis mandzijas,
vino el maromero,   me jevó a la iža.

—Venga otro maromero,   se jevi a la mía,
24 ¡ižo de re de Francia,   re de India!

(Saru, [wife of] Moše Papo)

15. *La princesa y el segador* (MP 108)
+ *Delgadina*(MP 99)

El buen rej tiene una iža,   una iža, una iža regalada.
Metióla en altas tores,   por tenelda, por tenelda bien guardada.
De komer no li deš nada,   más ke karne, más ke karne bien salada.
De biver no li deš nada,   más ke sumo, más ke sumo de naranđa.
5 Un día, de las kalores,   aparóse, aparóse a la ventana.
Vido a la rena su madre   en sija d'oro, en sija d'oro asentada.

—Así biva la rena mi madre,   ke mi dé, ke mi dé una gota d'agua.
8 Ke de set a el Alto do la alma. . . .

Note by the editors of *Jevrejski Glas*: "The ballad which we publish today is incomplete. This is apparent from the text itself, but we were also told of this by the person who sent it to us. We publish it in the hope that some of our readers will probably know other parts of it, which are omitted here, and that they will send them to us."

16. *Vos labraré un pendón* (MP 120)

—Ken kere tomar konsežo,   ke venga akí jo le daré:
ken kere gozar mansevo,   ki no se kaze a la vižés.
Digo jo, por miz pekados,   ke me kazí di trentaiséš.
Mi djeron una senjora   ke no tenía dizwséš.
5 Eja era una mužer pompoza,   jo un ombre gastador.
Gastí lo míjo i lo sujo   i lo ke el su padre muz djo.
Agora, por miz pekados,   jo me izi enkargador.
Eja avría la lana;   jo enkargava el algudón.
Tome esta lana blanka   i avrilda bjen delgada,
10 ke ansí está enkomendada   di el patrón ke me la djo.
—A mí non me parjó mi madre   porke avra lana jo,
sinon miz manikas blankas   lavrar seda i klavidón.
—A mí non mi parjó mi madre   para ke seja enkargador,
sinon miz manikas blankas   pezar seda i klavidón.
15 —Vajga él, el mi do marido,   a la kaša del kantón.
Ají tengo sjen dublones   ki mi kedó de mi senjor.
Mérkime seda di Brusa   i klavidón de Stambol
para lavrar laz miz ansjas,   ansjas del mi korasón.
De un kavo lavro la luna   i del otro lavro el sol,
20 en medjo de la tuvaža,   ansjas del mi korasón.
Si lu konto a mi padre,   mi deskaza a mí de voz.
Si lu konto a mi madre,   nos aborese a todos dos.
Si lu konto a mi ermano,   kun plomo muz da a todos dos.
24 Agora, por mis pekados,   lo entero en mi korasón.

(J. Katan)

23b   *See note to No. 8, 13b.*

Commentary by the editors of *Jevrejski Glas* (printed following text No. 19): "In spite of proofreading, some printing errors crept into the last two issues. For instance, in the first ballad (*Ken kere tomar konsežo*), *ki* was written instead of *ke* in several places.... [V. 15a] should read 'Vajga él, el mi marido.' We hope that the reader will correct other minor, mostly orthographic errors for himself."

17. *La doncella guerrera* (MP 121)

Prigoneros van i vjenen   por la sivdad d'Anadol:
todo el ke ižo varón tjene   a la gera lo mandó.
Ají uvía un vježo,   anjos tjene očentaidós,
bendizjendo al pan i al vino   i al Dio ke si lo dio;
5 maldizjendo a la su espoza   ke siete ižas li parió,
. . . .   i ni un ižo varón.
Saltó la más čika i dišo: . . . .
—No maldiga, il mi padre,   no maldiga, il mi senior.
Démi armas i kavajos,   a la gera mi vo jo.
10 —Las tus karikas, mi iža,   no demostran de varón.
—Las mi[s] karikas, mi padre,   il sol pretas mi las fazerá.
—Los tus kavejos, mi iža,   no demostran de varón.
—Los mi[s] kavejos, mi padre,   kon čapejo los tapo jo.
—Los tus pečikos, mi iža,   no demostran de varón.
15 —Los mi[s] pečikos, mi padre,   kon il [džak]et los tapo jo.
Tomó arma i kavajo,   a la gera eja partió.
Gerijando i pelijando,   il čapejo le kajó.
Il ižo de re ke la vido,   namorar se namoró.
—¿ Kén es, padre, este gere[ro]   ke la gera ja ganó ?
20 Esti gerero, mi padre,   iža es i varón no.
—Un konbite aziremos,   a él lo konbidaremos.
22 Aprevar lo aprevaremos;   si iža salió, tu eskoza sería.

(V. Altarac)

3a   uvía: *read* avía.
6a, 7b *We supply dots to indicate missing hemistichs.*
11a, 13a, 15a   *mi*[s]: *originally* mi.
15b, 19a *Type is damaged or worn away.*

18. *La vuelta del hijo maldecido* (MP 124)

—¿ Lo ke joráš, Blanka Njinja?   ¿ Lo ke joráš, Blanka Flor?
¿ O joráš por el mal prenjado,   o joráš por la mueva amor?
—No joro jo por el mal prenjado,   ni no joro por la mueva amor.
Joro jo por vos, kavajero,   ke voš vaš i me dešáš.
5 Me dešáš njinja i močaća,   a la flor de mi gozar.
Ja ke vos vaš, kavajero,   dešájme donde gastar.
Enkašó su mano al pećo,   sjen deblones li hue a dar.
—¿ Ké me daš esto, kavajero,   ke no mi abasta ni para pan?
Dos ežikas čikas tengo,   joran i demandan pan.
10 —Si esto no vos abasta,   ja tenéš donde gastar.
Venderéš kampos i vinjas,   media parte de sivdad.
—Ja ke vos vaš, kavajero,   dezíme kvándo tornáš.
—Si a los očo no torno,   a los mueve vos kazáš.
Tomaréš un manseviko,   ke seja me parignual.
15 Todos los mis vestidos,   ke le vajga a mí dad.
Esto ke sentió su madre,   maldisjón li hue ečar:
—Naves do todo el mundo   vajgan i ke tornen en pas
i la nave de su ižo   vajge i no torne más.
—No maldiga, la me madre,   jo so su ižo kar[ona]l.
20 Todo lo ke huera dičo,   esto era por burlar.

(Rifka, widow of H. Avram Atijas)

4b   voš: *read* vos.
14b   parignual: *read* parigual.
15b   *Text is corrupt.*
17a   do: *read* de.
18b   vajge: *read* vajga.
19b   *Type is blurred.*

19. *El encuentro del padre* (MP 125)

Kaminí por altas tores,   navigí por las fortunas.
Kají en tjeras aženas,   onde no me konosíjan,
onde no kantavan gajos,   ni menos kantan gajinas.
Ají el león abramava,   la leona respondía:
5 —¿ Ké buškas, ižo de ombre,   ké buškas por estas vinjas?
—Buško jo al re mi padre,   la korona ke él teníja.
—Kuando ja lo buškaríjas,   ¿ ké senjas de él me daríjas?
—Anjos tenía sisenta,   la barva blanka tenía.
9 —Por las senjas ke daríjas,   el re turko lo mataríja.

(Aron Abinun)

20. *El chuflete* (MP 142)

Salir kere el mez de mart,　entrar kere el mez de april,
kuando el rej de Alemanja　a Fráncija se kižo ir.
Kon sí jeva ðente munća,　kavajeros más de mil.
Djo el ćuflet a uno de sus mosos,　no lo supo sanergir.
5 Lo tomó el rej en su boka,　lo enpesó a sanergir.
La barka ke está en fortuna,　el porto la izo venir.
La parida ke está pariendo,　sin dolor la izo parir.
La kreatura ke está en kama,　sin tetar la izo dormir.
La puerta ke está serada,　sin jave la izo avrir.
10 El novjo ke a la novja ama,　a su kaza la izo venir.
—¡O, bien aga tal ćuflet　[i] los dublones ke di por ti!
12 Sien dublones más me kosta　[de las féridas] de Budim.

(Rabbi Mordehaj Z. Konforte)

6b　el: *read* al.
11b　*Type is damaged or worn away.*
12b　*Only tops of letters are legible; our reading is reasonably certain.*

Note by the editors of *Jevrejski Glas*: "From the collection of Rabbi Mordehaj Z. Konforte. In this issue we publish one more song from the collection of Mr. Mordehaj Konforte." This is the only *romance* contributed by Mordehaj Konforte; nor is this name connected with any of the lyric songs included in Rabbi Gaon's clippings. It is possible that Mordehaj Konforte and Moric Konforte (see No. 5) are the same individual. Mordehaj could simply be the Hebrew equivalent of Moric. If, on the other hand, this is not the case, it seems likely that some of the materials printed in *Jevrejski Glas* have not been preserved.

21. *La conversa*

Día di vjernis di manjanika,   ja si va ondi el pašá,
ke li dé la lisensia   ke turka si va aboltar.
Día di alhad di manjanika,   ja si va ondi el haham,
ke li dé la lisensia   ke turka si va aboltar.
5 Mandan a jamar padre i [madre],   ke li dé la lisensia,
ke li dé la lisensia   ke turka se va aboltar.
—¡Ajde, iža, ajde, kerida,   ajde, torna en tešuá!
Jo ti tomaré riku i franko,   ke pareska paregual.
—Jo no kero ni riko ni franko,   ni ki pareska paregual.
10 Ke la alma tengo apegada   kon el ižo de el pašá.
—Ajde, ižos, ajde, keridos,   asintemos en ješivá.
Komeremos pasas pretas,   ke a Bea la van a entarar.
Enterada ke la veja   a Beíka de onor:
tuvjendo todo bueno en kaza,   turka si hue a aboltar.
15 —Non si sikleje, mi madre,   ni si tome zehorá.
Aminjana es el đuzgo,   kon revólver le vo dar.
—Ni me darás, ni me tokarás,   ni me ozas a matar,
18 ke jo tengo siete letras   de el ižo de el pašá.

2a *Following No. 11, the editors of* Jevıejski Glas *call attention to a "printing error" in the present text: v. 2a should read* ke li korti feredžé di panjo.
5a *Type is damaged or worn away; the entire word is missing.*
16a Aminjana: *read* Amanjana.

ENGLISH ABSTRACTS AND NOTES

A1, B1, C3. *Virgilios* (MP 46): Virgil, in his medieval role as a womanizer, is imprisoned (without food or drink: B) for making love to Zadé (Zaïdé: B, Sadé: C), the king's niece **(Q433.5)**. Time passes and no one remembers him (except his mother, who visits him every day: BC). One day the king, on his way to mass (at mass: B; at the window: C), sees a woman pass by dressed in mourning. He is informed that it is Virgil's mother. He orders all his knights to finish saying mass quickly (and sit down to dinner, after which they will go to see Virgil. The queen refuses to eat without him: B). They all go to visit Virgil in prison. The king inquires as to Virgil's condition and is told that his beard, which had just begun to grow when he entered prison, is now turning grey. Virgil has been in prison seven years, yet he patiently offers to stay for sixteen (or ten: BC). The king summons his knights and they take Virgil off to the baths, after which he is given the royal crown (or the king's horses: C) and is married to the king's niece. / For bibliography of other Judeo-Spanish versions, see Attias 7, Bénichou 25 (pp. 99–102), NSR, pp. 64, 76. See also our "New Collection," p. 138. Pulido's version ("de Oriente") is almost certainly from Bosnia (pp. 295–297). Archaic text: *Primavera* 111.

A2, B15. *Rico Franco* (MP 85): The king has a daughter whom he will not exchange for gold, goods, or the riches one can count in an entire month; however, he wagers her at chess **(N2.6.2)**. None can win her. Moro Franco plays and wins her **(R10.1)**. Blanca Niña begins to cry. "Why are you crying? If you are crying for your father, he is now my cook (my jailer: B) **(L410.5)**; if for your mother, she is my washerwoman (my cook: B); if for your brothers, I have killed all three of them (and have tortured the youngest to death **[S161, S180; S112, K955]**. They sit down to dine: B). Blanca Niña asks for his knife to cut off her tresses, so she can send them to her father. She thrusts the knife into her abductor's heart (waist: B) **(J642, K631, K818, K818.1, K910)**. / For other Sephardic versions of this distant congener of *Lady Isabel and the Elf-Knight*, see Attias 9, Bénichou 37 (pp. 160–163), DRH 9, NSR, pp. 63–64, *nn.* 13–15, Yoná 18. Archaic text: *Primavera* 119.

A3, B16. *Silvana* (MP 98): Silvana is strolling along, playing a golden guitar and singing ballads. Her father, the king, falls in love with her, saying she is more beautiful in her everyday dress than is the queen, her mother, dressed in fine silk. He asks her to be his mistress (**T410, T411, T411.1**). Silvana asks who will suffer the torments of hell for her if she consents. Her father answers that he will. She protests that she must bathe first (**K1227.1**) and goes off crying to heaven for justice. Her mother hears her cries and asks to know what is troubling her. After the queen reassures her, they exchange dresses and the queen instructs Silvana to beg the king not to light candles that night. (The queen, in Silvana's stead [**K1223.2.1; K1317.5**] sleeps with the king, thus saving him from sin.) / A's text is corrupt at a number of points: *'enfermo* (v. 10; 'sick') is substituted for *infierno* ('hell') in an apparent attempt to de-Christianize the text. The imperfect character of vv. 11–12 may reflect avoidance of a reference to the pope, who appears in Peninsular versions at this point. In vv. 30ff., the text becomes impenetrably obscure, due probably to euphemistic tendencies which so often characterize Judeo-Spanish balladry. For other Sephardic texts, see Attias 41; NSR, pp. 64, *n.* 16, 77; Yoná 20. Although no sixteenth- and seventeenth-century texts have survived, there are early citations of the ballad's initial verse which attest to its popularity in the archaic tradition. See Yoná 20.

A4. *La infanta deshonrada* ("The Dishonored Princess;" MP 106): The princess has secretly given birth to an infant daughter (**T640**). She feigns illness and sends for her lover, the count, telling him to take the child away with him. As he is leaving he meets the king, who asks what he is carrying under his clothing. "Almonds," answers the count. The king asks for some to give to the princess, who is ill. The count refuses: "They have already been counted." The infant begins to cry. The count is accused of treason; some recommend that he be killed (**Q256; Q411**); others that he be married. He is married to the princess. / The ballad is scarce in the East; our Bosnian text is a precious rarity. Bibliography: Attias 23; Bénichou 3 (pp. 77–80); NSR, pp. 71–72. The Judeo-Spanish versions combine two sixteenth-century text-types: *Primavera* 159 (in *i-a*) and 160 (in *á-a*).

A5, B13, C19. *El encuentro del padre* ("The Father-Quest"; MP 125): Text A tells the following story: The protagonist sails before a storm and is thrown upon a foreign shore, where he is a stranger to all, where no cocks crow, where wolves howl and are answered by a lioness, where there is no cold or freezing water (*sic*). Twelve counts pass by and ask what he is doing there alone. "I'm looking for my brother" (**H1385.8**). They ask for a description. "He is as tall as a pine tree, as straight as an arrow, twenty-four years old, with a red beard."

They tell him his brother has been thrown into a well **(Q465.3, S146.1)**. B and C begin the same way; lions roar and are answered by the lioness, which apparently speaks (?) to the protagonist, asking him what he is doing **(B211.2.2)**. He is looking for his father, the king **(H1385.7)** and the king's crown; request for description. "He is seventy, with a white beard." "The Turkish king has ordered him killed" **(Q411)**. The son mourns for his father, tearing his clothing **(P678.1)**. Wiener 12 (also from Bosnia), the only other published text, is similar to B and C, except that the boy meets "two of the greatest generals in Turkey," who inform him of his father's death and take him to "a dark, ominous forest," where he mourns for his father. / The ballad is altogether enigmatic. We know of no Peninsular analogs. Its possible relationship to some unknown Castilian epic narrative or perhaps to some Balkan myth of the hero's unsuccessful father-quest remains a tantalizing problem. See D. E. Bynum, "Themes of the Young Hero in Serbo-croatian Oral Epic Tradition," *PMLA*, 83 (1968), 1296–1303.

B1: See A1.

B2, C6. *Conde Olinos* ("The Persecuted Lovers"; MP 55): The queen asks her daughter to come to her chamber at night and hear the mermaid's **(B81)** beautiful singing. The daughter answers: "It is not the mermaid, but rather a young man who is courting me. He can court me night and day but he shall not win me." The mother orders him killed **(T80)**, his body burned, and the ashes thrown into the sea. This will produce fine pearls and good coral **(D233, D237)**. The girl rushes to save him. She turns into a dove, he into a hawk **(E613, E613.6, E613.3)**. They fly off and alight on "the mansions of the Pasha." There is a "thorn tree" there which "will not let them rejoice." They then fly to "the mansions of the Vizier," but the "thorn tree will not let them live." / These Bosnian versions of the Pan-Hispanic *Conde Olinos* are strangely aberrant and incomplete. See Attias 16; Bénichou 28 (pp. 123–128); NSR, p. 77; Yoná 12. See also D. Levy Lida, pp. 63–64. Traces of an archaic text exist as a contamination in *El conde Arnaldos*. See H. A. Rennert, "Lieder des Juan Rodríguez del Padrón," *ZRPh*, XVII (1893), 544–558: p. 549 (MS version, vv. 19–32); Menéndez Pidal, "Poesía popular...," *Los romances de América*, pp. 65–68.

B3, C2. *Hero y Leandro* ("Hero and Leander"; MP 41): Of three sisters, two are married and the youngest is "in perdition." Her father, out of shame, sends her to France and builds her a stone castle in the middle of the sea **(R41.2, T50.1.2)**. Her lover finds out and throws himself into the sea, swimming and calling to Cara-de-flor (Blanca-flor: C). She is asleep, but recognizes his voice and throws down her tresses so he can climb up **(F843.1; F848.1)**. She gives him a change of clothes, dinner, and they go to bed. / The ballad is limited to the Eastern Sephardim and probably stems from a Greek treatment of the Pan-European Hero and Leander theme (*Die zwei Königskinder* [DVM, I, No. 20]) **(T83)**. See our "New Collection," pp. 141–142 (No. 17), Attias 61, and NSR, p. 78, for other versions.

B4, C1, vv. 10–17. *La choza del desesperado* ("The Hopeless Lover's Hermitage"; MP 140): The protagonist speaks to her (or his?) mother, threatening to go out and live in the fields **(T80, T93.2)**, eat grass, and drink her own tears; she will build a castle and invite in every passer-by. They will exchange accounts of their misfortunes. If those of the passer-by are greater, the protagonist will be patient; if hers are greater, she will throw herself down from the castle **(T93.3)**. / The ballad is exclusively Eastern, extremely popular, and uniform in its readings. See Attias 48, NSR, p. 77, and our "Hispanic Balladry," No. 6. Levy's version (No. 12), similarly combined with *Melisenda insomne*, as in C1 and Mrs. Crews' unedited text, must also be from Bosnia.

B5, C15, vv. 1–2, 5. *La princesa y el segador* ("The Princess and the Harvest Man"; MP 108): The king has an only daughter, whom he keeps guarded in a high tower **(R41.2, T50.1.2, T381)**. On a hot day she sits at the window, paring an apple. Some harvesters pass by **(T91, T91.6.4)**. She asks them to "gather her wheat and [reap] her barley" **(T55, T55.1)**. The harvester takes up residence with the girl **(T91)**. The king summons him (B should read: "Mandóle llamar el rey su padre"), but it takes him three weeks to make the eight-day journey to see the king. B is truncated; vv. 9–10 are a nontraditional accretion. The Sephardic texts usually abbreviate or attenuate events subsequent to the girl's request, while the vastly popular Peninsular versions are often openly obscene. / Bibliography: Attias 90; NSR, p. 78; SICh 9. For a selection of Peninsular versions see SICh, pp. 379–380, *n.* 15.

B6, C7: *La vuelta del marido* (*i*; "The Husband's Return"; MP 58): Amadí's lady sits combing her hair with a crystal (ivory: C) comb on the highest branch of a marvelous tree **(F811)** (B asserts that the lady *is* the smallest branch of the tree), which has golden roots and a base of ivory **(F811.1.1, F811.1.7; N711.1)** (C, v.4 belongs between vv. 1 and 2). A knight, who looks like Amadí, passes by (and asks what she is looking for: C) **(N711.1)**. She asks him if he has seen Amadí. He knows him well and claims to have a letter for her from Amadí (cf. **K1349.2**). He asks what she would give in exchange for Amadí. In B she offers three doubloons. He asks for something more. She offers her three tresses. He asks for something more. She offers three mills, which grind pepper, ginger (?), and white flour, and her three daughters to serve and amuse the knight. (In C she offers her three fields of wheat, ginger, and white wheat. He wants more. She offers three mills, grinding clove, ginger, and white flour. He wants more. She offers her three daughters to serve and sleep with the knight.) He will only settle for possessing her. She curses him. He then identifies himself as Amadí **(H1556, H1556.2)**. He asks her for some sign of identification and she tells him that he has a "blue mole" under his left breast **(H51.1)** (in C these verses, usually spoken by the wife, should come after v. 23). He tells her to throw down her tresses so he can use them to climb up to her **(F843.1, F848.1)**. / Jungić's second musical example (appended to Baruch's article) also represents this ballad. Wiener collected another Bosnian version (No. 8); Levy's text (No. 7) is probably also from Bosnia. For other Judeo-Spanish versions and Peninsular congeners, see Attias 20, NSR, pp. 70–71, *n.* 44. There are genetically related Provençal, French, and French Canadian analogs: Arbaud, I, 162–165; Davenson 52; Decombe, pp. 214–216; Rolland, I, 220–223; Barbeau, *Rossignol*, pp. 19–20; Gagnon, *Chansons populaires du Canada*, pp. 51–52.

B7. *La vuelta del marido* (*á-a*; "The Husband's Return"): The queen is seated in her garden stringing pearls with a golden needle. A knight, who looks like her husband, passes by. She asks if he has seen her husband, Montesico of France. He has seen him, knows him, and bears a letter from him: "She should look for another husband, for he has found another lady" **(H1556)**. The queen utters a cry of sorrow which pierces the heavens and makes the earth tremble. He tells her not to cry; he is Montesico of France. She curses any woman who would trust a man. / This unique text is genetically related to a ballad well known in, but seemingly limited to, the Catalan linguistic domain, where its initial verses are often contaminated by *¿ Por qué no cantáis la bella?* (MP 57), just as is B7, vv. 1–2. For Catalan versions, see AFC 2307; Aguiló, pp. 83–90; Avenç, I, 31–34; Briz, II, 191; Bulbena, pp. 36–39; Capmany 14; Llorens 26–27; Milá 202; OCPC, I, 111, 122–123, II, 304, III, 238, 262–263.

B8. *Landarico* (MP 82): The king sets out to go hunting but goes to the queen's quarters instead. He finds her combing her hair with a golden comb and a crystal mirror in her hand. To joke with her he strikes

her with a stick. She answers: "Be still, Andarleto, my fine lover
(K1550.1). I have two sons by you, and two more by the king, which
makes four **(T230, T481)**. The king's sons go to war; yours stay by
my side. The king's sons ride mules; yours ride both mules and horses.
The king's sons sleep on feathers; yours sleep at my side." She turns
around and finds the king beside her: "Pardon, pardon, Lord King, for
what I have said! I dreamt it all last night at midnight!" **(K1500)**.
"I'll pardon you, my Queen, with your head to one side" **(Q411.0.1,
Q421.0.2)**. Vv. 16–17 are out of context. They are a survival of a con-
versation between Landarico and the queen which is present in the
sixteenth-century version. Cf. Wiener 11. / Bibliography: Attias 36;
Bénichou 8 (pp. 103–108); DRH 6; NSR, p. 77. Wiener 11 is from
Bosnia. Cf. also Levy, No. 14. Archaic text: ASW 46–47.

B9. *Bernal Francés* (MP 83): The queen is sewing in her garden
with a golden needle and an ivory fan (?). She hears a knock at the
door and goes to open it. On entering, the "Pilgrim," who is her husband disguised as her lover, blows out the candle **(K1550.1; K1817.2)**.
She asks him why he has done this. He claims that his eyes hurt.
She takes him up stairs, washes his hands and feet, sets a golden table
for him where the king usually eats, and makes him a feather bed
where the king usually sleeps. At midnight he does not turn toward
her. She asks him why he is acting so strangely and assures him that,
if it is for fear of the king, he is far away **(T230, T481)**, and that
she hopes to hear news that he has been killed by lions. He answers
that, when morning comes, he will cut for her a fine dress with a
scarlet neckpiece **(Q411.0.1, Q421.0.2)**: "Call the Pilgrim to save you;
call your parents to save you." When morning came, he cut a fine
dress for her. / Bibliography: Danon 24. See J. B. Avalle-Arce's fundamental study, "Bernal Francés y su romance," *AEM*, III (1966),
327–391. The wish that the husband be killed by lions (v. 15 of Baruch's
text) is borrowed from some version of *La adúltera* (ó). Cf. C12, v.2.

B10, C9: *Parto en lejas tierras* ("Death from Childbirth in a Distant
Land"; MP 68): A young woman, about to give birth in a foreign
land, yearns for the presence of her mother. She begs her husband
to ask *his* mother for help. On hearing this plea, the girl's mother-
in-law sows her garden with salt: "When this salt sprouts flowers,
my daughter-in-law will go into labor. When it sprouts leaves, may she
be among the fortunate (read *dičozas*)" **(D1039.2, D1782, S51.1,
T574)**. The son answers: "If you were not my mother and were
instead my stepmother, I would remove your head with this sword
of mine!" He returns to his house and tells his wife that she must give

birth alone, for his mother was not at home. She begs him to go in search of *her* mother. On being told of the approaching birth, the girl's mother goes to the henhouse: "May my daughter give birth with the same ease as the hens" **(D1782, D1501.2)**. The mother goes to her daughter's aid, but along the way she hears the tolling of a sad and bitter bell **(V115)**. On inquiring about its meaning, she is told that it is tolling for a girl who died in childbirth. She throws herself down from a mountain top **(N344)**. Baruch's very imperfect fragment (B10) supplies the hero's traditionally authentic name: *Don Beso* (read *Bezo*) or *Bueso*. Jungić's first musical example (appended to Baruch's collection) represents this same text-type. / Though it contains a number of seven- and eight-syllable verses, the ballad is essentially in parallelistic *romancillo* (six-syllable) couplets and shares this metrical peculiarity with its Peninsular analogs. It is extremely rare in the Sephardic East. We have some fragments and one reasonably complete version from Rhodes. C9 is to be considered the first complete Eastern Judeo-Spanish version to reach print, since Danon 5 (only the last 16 hemistichs) and Molho's almost identical text (*Literatura*, pp. 74–75, No. 7, vv. 22–28) are mere fragments appended to *El sueño profético* (see B19; also our "New Collection," pp. 138–139). We know of only one Moroccan example (Larrea 92), which like unedited texts from Tetuán and Alcazarquivir in our collection, is certainly a recent Peninsular importation. The ballad enjoys a wide distribution in the center and west of the Peninsula and even reaches Brazil. Castilian: ART 222–223; CPE, II, 46; Fernández-Núñez, *Folk-lore leonés*, No. 3 (music, Nos. 59, 151); Güéjar 9; RPC 43–46; RPM 156–157; RTCN 125. See also the fragment cited in MP 68. Galicia: Carré 66, Sampedro 181. Portugal: Braga, I, 573–577; Furtado de Mendonça, *RL*, XIV, 4–6; Nunes, *RL*, VI, 185–187; Reis Dâmaso, pp. 171–173; Tavares, *RL*, VIII, 78; Vasconcellos, "Bibl. do Povo," pp. 58–60; VRP 552–553. Brazil: Braga, I, 582–584; Pereira da Costa, pp. 331–333; S. Romero, No. 14 (the notes confuse the ballad with *La mala suegra* [MP 70]). *El parto en lejas tierras* shows undeniable similarities, if not genetic relationship, to a cluster of Central European ballads: the German *Elfjährige Markgräfin* (DVM, II, No. 53) and its Yiddish (Mlotek, pp. 213 f.) and Slovenian (DVM, II, 290) analogs. More distant is the analogy with Child's *Fair Mary of Wallington* (No. 91). All of these ballads share a general narrative outline with our Hispanic poem: The girl is married in a distant land (DVM/ Slov.); on feeling birth pangs, she sends for her mother (DVM/Yiddish/Slov./Child); the husband carries the message (DVM/Yiddish); as the mother approaches she hears church bells (DVM/Slov.); she asks a shepherd for whom they are tolling (DVM); the girl has died or dies in childbirth (DVM/

Yiddish/Slov./Child). Notable is the intervention of the mother-in-law, who in the Yiddish ballad "refuses to summon a midwife or alleviate her daughter-in-law's agony in any way" (Mlotek, p. 213). The Hispanic, English, and Central European ballads embody motifs of a very universal character; their possible genetic relationship remains in doubt, but it is certainly worthy of further study. The obvious sympathetic magic practiced by the mother-in-law is unique in our Bosnian version, being found in no other text in the Hispanic tradition (elsewhere the mother-in-law simply curses the girl or wishes that she die of a hemorrhage). The clearly magical sowing of salt by the mother-in-law, if not the mother's countermeasure, is reminiscent of another Northern European ballad-type, represented by *Willie's Lady* (Child 6) and the Scandinavian *Hustru og Mands Moder* (DgF, II, No. 84). Here the mother-in-law, by sympathetic or symbolic magical means, casts a spell on the girl, by which she is unable to give birth. However, these ballads usually end happily when "nine witch knots," "kaims o'care," and other magical impediments are removed and the girl is immediately delivered **(T582.3)**. Needless to say, the similarity to our Bosnian text implies no genetic relationship.

After the present book was in final form, we received from our friend Professor Moshe Attias his article on *El parto en lejas tierras*, "Reconstrucción de una romansa sefardía" (in Hebrew), *Tesoro de los judíos sefardíes*, XI–XII (Jerusalem, 1969–1970), 46–51. The version given to Attias by Dr. Samuel Pinto of Sarajevo is identical to that of *Jevrejski Glas* and must be based directly on it. Note at the lacuna in v. 34, where we supply *gajinas*, Attias' version reads *aves*, which is the only significant difference between the two texts.

B11, C4. *Hermanas reina y cautiva* ("The Queen and the Captive Who Were Sisters"; MP 48): The queen sends her Moorish raiders to France to capture a slave girl, "not of lowly birth but related to dukes and counts and of a fine family" **(R10.1)**. The queen and the captive are both with child and give birth on the same day. The queen bears a daughter; the captive a son. The midwives switch the children **(K1847, P313.1)**. One day the queen overhears the captive singing to the infant girl: "If you were my daughter, I would call you Marqueta (Flor-de-las-flores: C), which was my sister's name." The sisters are reunited **(H12)**. [They determine to return to their Christian homeland.] The captive consoles the queen: "If you have lost the king, I will marry you to a duke" (B, vv. 23–24). / Bibliography: Attias 11; Bénichou 13 (pp. 219–226); NSR, p. 77. The ballad, known also in the Peninsular tradition, is a very distant relative of *Fair Annie* (Child 62) and its Germanic analogs, although in other features it is clearly linked to the story of *Floire et Blanceflor*. See Bénichou, pp. 220–221.

B12, C18. *La vuelta del hijo maldecido* ("The Accursed Son's Return"; MP 124): Blanca Niña laments her husband's departure. She asks him for money with which to feed her three children. He gives her a hundred doubloons. She says they will not be enough. In that case, he says, she should sell fields, vineyards, and half of the city. She asks him when he will return. "If I do not return in eight years, marry on the ninth year (cf. **T61.2**). Marry a young man who must be my equal. All my clothing should fit him exactly. When his mother hears this, she sets a curse upon him: "May all the ships in the world come and go in peace. May my son's ship go forth and never return" (**M411.1**). Time passes. A boat passes by. The mother asks a knight in the boat if he has seen her son. "Indeed I have seen him and know him; he is lying on a sand bank. A hawk can go in and out of every one of his wounds" (**K1860**). The mother tries to throw herself into the sea (**F1041.1.2.2.4, N344**), but the knight, who is her son, reveals his true identity. C's final verse: "It was all a joke," is an inept, nontraditional addition. B, v.2, and C, vv. 2–3, represent a contamination from *La adúltera* (*ó*), although the pertinent verses do not occur in C12. Cf. Yoná, No. 8, *n.* 5. / Bibliography: Attias 24; NSR, p. 77; Yoná 23; our "New Collection," pp. 142–146. The ballad combines the archaic *romance* of *Conde Dirlos* (*Primavera* 164) with a story originating in the Greek song *Hē kakè mána* ("The Evil Mother"). See our "New Collection," *loc. cit.*

B13: See A5.

B14, C17. *La doncella guerrera* ("The Girl Who Went to War"; MP 121): We follow the verse order of B: Knights (criers: C) go about through the city of Aragón (Anatolia: C): "Anyone who does not have a son will be sent to the wars himself." An old man, doubled over with age (eighty-two years: C), was there (passed by: C). He was blessing the bread, and the wine, and God, who gave them to him; he was cursing his wife, who had given birth to seven daughters and not one son. The youngest daughter, who was born with good fortune, jumped up and said: "Do not curse, my father, do not curse, my lord. Give me arms and a horse; I will go to the wars for you." "My daughter, do not say such a dishonorable thing. Your beautiful bosom proves you are not a man." "I will cover my bosom with my coat." "Your beautiful tresses prove you are not a man." "I will cover them with my hat." "Your beautiful complexion (cheeks: C) proves you are not a man." "The wind and the sun will make me lose it (will blacken my cheeks: C)." She took arms and a horse and man's clothing and went off to war **(K1837, K1837.6)**. Messengers come and go [saying] that she had won half the war. As she was waging war and fighting, her hat fell off. When the king's son saw her, he fell in love: "What can I tell you, my mother, about what happened to me today? A young man who came to the wars is a girl and not a man" ("Who is this warrior, my father, who won the war? This warrior is a girl and not a man." "We will invite him to a feast": C). [In other versions, the girl is subjected to a series of tests **(H1578, H1578.1)**, through which she passes successfully without betraying the fact that she is not a man.] / Bibliography: Attias 40; Bénichou 11 (pp. 175–179); NSR, p. 77. A number of Peninsular versions are brought together by F. de Castro Pires de Lima, *A mulher vestida de homem (Contribuição para o estudo do romance "A Donzela que vai à Guerra")*, [Coimbra], 1958. A study of the Hispanic ballad's strikingly close relationship to European forms is an important desideratum. As starting points see Poueigh, *Chansons populaires des Pyrénées françaises*, pp. 225–226; Nigra 48; DVM, V, No. 95; Leader, *Hungarian Classical Ballads*, pp. 344–346; Schirmunski, *Vergleichende Epenforschung*, pp. 104–105 (No. 4); Strausz, *Bulgarische Volksdichtungen*, pp. 131–134.

B15: See A2.

B16: See A3.

B17, C20. *El chuflete* ("The Magic Flute"; MP 142): The month of March is going out and April is coming in, when the wheat is in the grain and flowers about to bloom. Then the King of Germany set out for France. He took with him a great following, more than a thousand knights. He took with him a little flute from the fairs at Paris **(D1223.1, D1224, D1224.1, D1225)**. The king passed the flute from mouth to mouth; no one could make it sound (The king gave it to one of his servants, but he could not make it sound: C). "Accursed be such a flute and the doubloons I paid for it!" The king took it in his mouth and was able to make it sound **(D1275.1, D1275.2)**. It made all the ships in the world come to dry land **(D1523.2.6)**; it made the woman in labor give birth without pain **(D1501.2)**; it made the crying babe fall asleep without suckling; it made the girl who loves her suitor come to his side **(D1426.1)**. "Blessed be such a flute and the doubloons I paid for it!" ("It cost me a hundred doubloons more in the fairs of Budim": C). C includes variant marvels: "It made the boat sailing before the storm come into port **(D1523.2.6)**; it makes the closed door open without a key" **(D2088)**. / Bibliography: Attias 49; Yoná 27. MP 142, vv. 12–15, apparently from Vienna, are undoubtedly of Bosnian origin.

B18. *Morena me llaman*: "They call me dark, though I was born fair. From walking [in the sun], so gracefully, I lost my complexion. The king's son calls me dark. If he calls me again, I'll go with him." / This very popular Eastern Judeo-Spanish lyric song is also known on the Peninsula and can be documented in early *cancioneros* and Golden Age drama. Eastern Judeo-Spanish versions: Bassan 140; Estrugo, p. 132; Frenk Alatorre, *Lírica hispánica*, No. 599 (= D. Levy Lida); Levy, *Chants*, 21, 24; D. Levy Lida, pp. 65–67; Molho, *Literatura*, pp. 105–106; Pulido, p. 328; Wiener 13, 22. We have a number of unedited texts. Some Sephardic versions (Frenk Alatorre; Levy) include the couplet:

> Morenica a mí me llaman
> los marineros;
> si otra vez me llaman
> yo me vo con ellos.

The same verses occur in the Peninsular tradition (Rodríguez Marín, *Cantos*, II, 1438; see Pulido, p. 328, *n.* 1; Torner, *Lírica hispánica*, p. 40):

> Morenita resalada
> Me llaman los marineros;
> Otra vez que me lo digan,
> Me voy al muelle con ellos.

Torner cites an Argentine adaptation (*Lírica hispánica*, p. 40):

> Salteñito me dicen
> las santiaguesas;
> otra vez que me digan,
> me iré con ellas.

Lope de Vega's *Servir a señor discreto* ("Academia" ed., XV [Madrid, 1913], 590b) records a seventeenth-century form (see also Frenk Alatorre, "Supervivencias," p. 67; Lope de Vega, *Poesías líricas*, ed. J. F. Montesinos, 2 vols. [Madrid: "Clásicos Castellanos," 1968 and 1963], I, 84):

> Mariquita me llaman
> los arrieros;
> Mariquita me llaman,
> voyme con ellos.

The Sephardic song's initial couplet, concerning the girl's darkened complexion, is attested in various early song books:

> Aunque soy morena,
> blanca yo nací:
> guardando el ganado
> la color perdí.

See Frenk Alatorre, *Lírica hispánica*, No. 196 (from Biblioteca Nacional, Madrid, Ms 3915); id., "Supervivencias," p. 67; Torner, *Lírica hispánica*, p. 267; Cejador, *La verdadera poesía*, I, No. 778. On the defense of brunettes and dark girls in the primarily fair-complexion-oriented early lyric, see Cejador, I, Nos. 228, 232, 335, 929, 975; Frenk Alatorre, *Lírica hispánica*, Nos. 197–205; id., *La lírica popular*, pp. 44–45; Torner, Nos. 122, 157; A. Sánchez Romeralo, *El villancico* (Madrid, 1969), pp. 56–59. The theme is enormously popular in modern tradition. See Rodríguez Marín, II, Nos. 1404–1456, III, Nos. 4157–4158. See also Algazi, No. 74, and Kamhi, p. 118, for another Judeo-Spanish instance. See also Bruce W. Wardropper, "The Color Problem in Traditional Poetry," *MLN*, LXXXV (1960), 415–421.

B19. *El sueño profético* ("The Prophetic Dream"; MP 68, 129): The Queen of France had three daughters. One was embroidering, the other was sewing, the youngest was embroidering on a frame. (The youngest falls asleep and dreams an allegorical dream **[D1812.3.3, D1812.3.3.5]**. Her mother interprets it: She is to be married **[D1812.3.3.9]**.) / Bibliography: Attias 60; NSR, p. 78. See also our "New Collection," pp. 138–139 (No. 7) concerning the ballad's probable Greek source.

B20. *Morenico sos*: "You are dark, my love. To me you are a rose. You deceived many girls; my love turned out true." / We know of no other published version of this lyric song, which we have, however, heard in oral tradition.

Jungić 1–3: Of the three *"romance"* tunes transcribed by Miss B. Jungić following Baruch's article, only two belong to narrative ballads. The first represents *Parto en lejas tierras* (see B10); the second is *La vuelta del marido* (*i*; see B6). The third text is a very popular lyric song: "In the sea there is a tower **(cf. R41.2)**; in the tower there is a window; in the window there is a dove, who loves (often *yama* 'calls to') the mariners." / For other versions, see Algazi 69–70; Elnecavé 18; Idelsohn, Nos. 490, 492; Kamhi, p. 118; Levy 33; D. Levy Lida, p. 69; Molho, *Literatura*, p. 100. Rodríguez Marín records an almost identical

Spanish version (IV, No. 8171). Concerning Miss Jungić's musical transcriptions, see Katz, *Judeo-Spanish Traditional Ballads from Jerusalem*, pp. 111–113, 197, *nn.* 117–119.

C1. *Melisenda insomne* ("Sleepless Melisenda"; MP 28): "Nights, nights, good nights, nights for loving! Oh, mother, I cannot stand this night, turning about in bed like a fish in the sea." "I have three little daughters all of the same age." The first one jumped up and said: "Let us enjoy our youth! Tomorrow we will be betrothed and there'll be no more time for joy." The second jumped up and said: "Let us enjoy our betrothal! Tomorrow we will be married and there'll be no more time for joy." The third jumped up and said: "Mother, how can I leave you?" / Bibliography: Attias 33; Bénichou 2 (pp. 69–76); NSR, pp. 65, *nn.* 19–20, 77. Archaic text: *Primavera* 198. The rest of C1 (vv. 10 ff.) is a version of *La choza del desesperado* (see B4). Cf. Levy, No. 12.

C2: See B3.

C3: See A1.

C4: See B11.

C5. *Don Bueso y su hermana* ("Don Bueso and His Sister"; MP 49): A girl is abducted by three Moors and carried off to a foreign realm **(R10.1)**. The Moorish queen claims that she does not want the captive, fearing the king will be attracted to the beautiful girl **(T257.1)**. She is deprived of wine in the hope that her beauty will fade, but she only becomes more beautiful under harsh treatment. She is sent to the river to wash clothes early in the morning. A knight rides by and asks her to go away with him **(N715.1)**. She asks what she should do with the clothes she has been washing. He tells her to take along the clothes of gold **(F821.1.1)** but to leave those of wool and silk in the river. As they ride along, she recognizes the fields of olive and pomegranate trees she knew as a child. The knight realizes that she is his sister. Their mother joyfully welcomes her long-lost daughter. / Bibliography: Attias 1; Bénichou 14 (pp. 239–241); DRH 8; NSR, p. 76. See also our "New Collection," p. 137 (No. 1). On the ballad's relationship to the Germanic *Meererin, Südeli*, and other Northern European ballads, see R. Menéndez Pidal's fundamental "Supervivencia del poema de *Kudrun* (Orígenes de la balada)," *RFE*, XX (1933), 1–59 (reprinted in *Los godos y la epopeya española* [Madrid, 1956], pp. 89–173), or "Das Fortleben des Kudrungedichtes (Der Ursprung der Ballade)," *JVF*, V (1936), 85–122.

C6: See B2.

C7: See B6.

C8. *La novia abandonada* ("The Abandoned Fiancée"; MP 67): On the way to evening prayer, the narrator meets a beautiful girl. He is unable to rest. [His mother (?)] asks him why he is restless. He tells of his encounter with the girl and says that he has asked her father and mother for her hand, but they have refused. He asks her brother and he attacks him. [The suitor leaves the girl and takes refuge in a distant land. The girl sets out in search of him (**H1385.5**), but finds that he has married someone else.] / The ballad is extremely rare in the East. Adatto (No. 13, vv. 1–18) has uncovered one version (from Turkey?); there is another from Rhodes in our unedited collection. The *Jevrejski Glas* text gives only the initial episode. The ballad is known in Morocco only as a contamination in *Catalina* (MP 67): Larrea 90, vv. 21 ff., 91, vv. 22 ff.; Ortega, p. 232. It enjoys a some-what more vigorous traditional life in Galicia, Portugal, and Brazil, although here it is usually contaminated with *Conde Olinos*: See Carré 19–20; Sampedro 169; VRP 249–256; Pereira da Costa, pp. 311–313; S. Romero, No. 4. See also Yoná 12, *n.* 21.

C9: See B10.

C10. *La malcasada del pastor* ("The Shepherd's Mismated Wife"; MP 72): The protagonist, a young girl, is married to a shepherd. After a month he puts her to a test (**H1556**). At midnight, he sends her on a tiring walk to a distant fountain to fetch water (**T35.1**). She falls asleep [by the fountain]. A knight passes by and gives her three kisses (**H1556.2**). The girl exclaims: "If my husband finds out, I will be killed." The knight identifies himself as "her beloved." / Bibliography: Bénichou 6 (pp. 134–137). See also our "New Collection," pp. 141–142 (No. 17). Wiener's version (No. 9) is of Bosnian provenance.

C11. *La mujer engañada* ("The Deceived Wife"; MP 74): The pro-tagonist's husband leaves her; she follows him to the house of a fair girl (**T230; T481**). The abandoned wife enters and sees fine food, beds with fine curtains, and her husband flirting with the girl. She returns home, locks her door with seven bolts (**Z71.5**), and consoles herself by singing a lullaby to her infant daughter concerning what she has seen. Her husband returns and asks to be admitted, saying that he has been working in his vineyards (**K1500**). She tells him that he has been with the other girl. The following morning she goes

to the Rabbi and asks, unwillingly, to be released from her marriage. /
Bibliography: Attias 43; Bénichou 7 (pp. 129–133); NSR, p. 77; Yoná
15. For archaic evidence, see Bénichou and Yoná.

C12. *La adúltera* (ó; "The Adulteress"; MP 78): The unfaithful
wife speaks [to her lover] saying that her husband, the king, has gone
to the wars in Anatolia; she hopes that the Moors may kill him so that
they can be married **(T230, T481)**. At this moment the king returns
and asks to be admitted, saying that the fine rain is soaking his jacket.
The wife answers that if the jacket is of cloth, she will make him
another of silk; if it is of silk, she will make another of silver thread.
The king becomes enraged and breaks down the door. He finds his
wife crying and asks why; she has lost the keys to the corridor **(K1500)**.
"If the keys are of iron," he says, "I will make you others of silver
[literally 'of silver cloth']." He then asks: "Whose is this horse that
I see?" She answers: "It was sent to you by my father so you could
win the war of Anatolia." "Whose are these shoes I see?" "They
were sent to me by my father so I could serve the king with all my
heart." "Whose are these arms which I see?" "My father sent them to
you so you could win the war of Anatolia." "Who is this I see in the
bed chamber?" **(K1550.1)**. "May eyes which see such a thing be
blinded!" He cuts off their hands and feet **(S180, S161)** and gives
them a cruel death **(Q411.0.1)**. / Bibliography: Attias 12; Bénichou
39 (pp. 142–144); Yoná 16, *n*. 11. Archaic texts: *Primavera* 136–136a.
On the ballad's European congeners, which include *Our Goodman*
(Child 274), see Yoná 16, *n*. 11.

C13A–13B. *La adúltera* (á-a; "The Adulteress"; MP 80): The husband asks Burjula who is knocking at the door so early. "It's just the
baker's boy who is asking me for leavening, though I do not even
have flour." She tells her husband to leave the house early: "Business
carried out in the morning is unequalled in (lasts for: 13B) the entire
week" **(K1500)**. As the husband goes out through the door, the lover
enters through the window **(T230, T481)**. Along the way, the husband realizes that he has forgotten his keys. He returns to the house
and asks his wife to open the door: "My feet are in the snow, my
head is in the frost" **(K1212)**. The wife answers: "How can I open
the door to you? I have my child in my lap and that wretch is in my
bed." (These verses are, of course, completely incongruous if spoken
to the husband; in most versions, they occur at the beginning of the
story and, like the reference to snow and frost, apply to the lover.)
The wife then puts her lover in a chest used to store pepper; he sneezes.
The husband asks who is sneezing. "It's the neighbor woman's cat

that is catching mice for us." The husband asks for the keys to the
box. "I lost them on wash day." "Go ask the neighbor's wife to lend
you hers." She says she does not dare, for this would lead to quarreling
between the neighbor and his wife. The husband siezes an axe and
splits open the box (K1550, K1550.1). He invites the neighbor women
in to see "a bearded cat with curled mustachioes" (cf. K1515). Moral:
"He who has a beautiful wife must take care to guard her well, for the
(red: 13B) cat will come along and carry her off, and he'll be left with
nothing." / Bibliography: Attias 58; NSR, pp. 73–74, *n.* 60, 78; Yoná
16. Levy's No. 85 is probably from Bosnia.

C14. *El raptor pordiosero* ("The Abductor in Beggar's Guise"); MP
92): The protagonist has unsuccessfully courted a girl for seven years
(Z71.5). He disguises himself as a pilgrim (K1817.1, K1817.2). ("Maromero de la ruina" was probably once 'mal romero de Roma' [cf. Danon
28], before the phrase became de-Christianized.) The girl's mother
tells her to give alms to the pilgrim. He squeezes her finger, telling
her that he is blind, and begs her to show him to the gates of the
castle. When they are alone outside, he embraces her, kisses her, and
sets her on his horse (R10.1). "I was wooed by dukes and counts
and now I have been deceived by an evil pilgrim" (T91). He answers:
"I am a duke and a count, son of the King of France, and King of
India." The mother laments to her neighbors that her daughter has
been carried off by a pilgrim. One of them answers: "Let another
pilgrim come and carry off *my* daughter, just so he's son of the King
of France and King of India." / Bibliography: Attias 44; Danon 28.
The ballad occurs in various Peninsular subtraditions: Castile (joined
to *La gentil porquera*), Galicia, and Portugal: See RPM 104–107;
Carré 25–29; Sampedro 188; VRP 517–532. The Catalan *Darideta*
(AFC 3213), Provençal *Liseto* (Arbaud, I, 133–138), and French–French
Canadian *La brune et le brigand* (Barbeau-Sapir, pp. 133–137; Gagnon,
pp. 144–146) are doubtless also related to the Spanish ballad. Other
Continental congeners are *La bella Leandra* (Nigra 43), *The Jolly Beg-
gar* and *The Beggar-Laddie* (Child 279–280).

C15, vv. 1–2 and 5 are from *La princesa y el segador*: See B5. The
rest of the text is a fragment of the incestuous ballad of *Delgadina*
(MP 99): [Delgadina's father attempts to seduce her (T410, T411,
T411.1). When she rejects his advances, he has her imprisoned (Q433,
R41).] She is to be given only salted meat and [bitter] orange juice
(Q501.7.1). She looks out of a window and sees her mother seated on a
golden chair. She begs to be given a drop of water, for she is about to
die of thirst. [The mother, then brothers and sisters, all refuse to help

her. Finally the father tells his servants to give her water, but at that moment she expires.] / Bibliography: Attias 45; Bénichou 43 (pp. 252–253); NSR, p. 77; Yoná 20, *n.* 3.

C16. *Vos labraré un pendón* ("I shall weave you a pennant"; MP 120): "Whoever wants advice, let him come to me and I'll give him some: Whoever wishes to enjoy himself as a young man should not marry in old age **(J445.2, T121)**. I speak for myself, for my sins, since I married when I was thirty-six. They married me to a lady who was not yet sixteen. She was an extravagant woman and I was a spendthrift man. I spent my money and hers and what her father had given us **(W131.1)**. And now, for my sins, I became a carder [of wool]. (The text erroneously reads 'a loader.') She opened the wool and I carded the cotton." [He speaks to his wife:] "Take this white wool and spread it out very thin, for this is what the master who gave it to me has ordered." "My mother did not bring me into this world to spread out wool; my fine little hands are for embroidering silk and golden thread" **(L113.1.0.1)**. He answers: "My mother did not give birth to me so I should be a carder; my fine hands are for weighing silk and golden thread." She tells him to go to the chest in the corner in which there are one hundred doubloons left over from her dowry: "Buy me silk from Brusa and golden thread from Istanbul, so that I can embroider the grief which is in my heart. At one end [of the cloth] I shall embroider the sun; at the other end, the moon; in the center I shall embroider the grief which is in my heart **(D1051)**. If I tell my father, he will separate me from you. If I tell my mother, she will loathe us both. If I tell my brother, he will attack us both. Now, for my sins, I will bury [my grief] in my heart." [Other versions end happily: The wife weaves a marvelous cloth **(D1051)**, which saves them from poverty when the king recognizes it as his daughter's handwork **(H110)**.] / Bibliography: Attias 47; Bénichou 9 (pp. 164–168); NSR, p. 77; Yoná 22. On the ballad's distant European analogs, see Yoná. Vv. 1–4 of C16 are a contamination from *Celinos y la adúltera*, concerning which see DRH 10, Yoná 17, and our "Romance de *Celinos y la adúltera* entre los sefardíes de Oriente," *ALM*, II (1962), 5–14. This contamination seems to be traditional in Bosnian versions of *Vos labraré un pendón* (cf. Levy, No. 67).

C17: See B14.

C18: See B12.

C19: See A5.

C20: See B17.

C21. *La conversa* ("The Renegade Girl"): On Friday morning, Bella goes to the pasha and asks to be allowed to become a Moslem. On Sunday morning, she goes to the rabbi and asks the same thing. They send for her parents and ask their permission. The father tells her: "Come on, dear daughter, repent! I will marry you to a rich European." "I don't want any rich European. My soul is attracted to the pasha's son." **(V331.5)**. The father calls his sons to the synagogue. They will sit and eat black raisins, for Bella is to be buried (that is, considered dead for having abandoned her religion). One of the sons (?) comforts the mother and threatens to kill Bella with a revolver. She remains steadfast: "You will not strike me, nor touch me, nor dare to kill me, for I have a document (lit. 'seven letters') from the son of the pasha."/ This humorous little ballad was obviously composed in the Balkans and probably at a rather recent date. Its perspective is curious, for it is so thoroughly Jewish in ambiance and vocabulary that one might have expected a condemnation of the girl on religious grounds. Instead, the ballad's sympathies are clearly on the side of the spirited girl who is willing to sacrifice all for the sake of love. The only parallel we know of is Levy's rather insipid text (No. 11), where the girl turns Turk simply because she has been punished for burning some stuffed grape leaves (*yaprakes*) that she was cooking. The theme of religious conversion is, however, of ancient provenience in the *Romancero* and, like our Sephardic song, is sometimes expressed, curiously enough, by a formula in *á-e* assonance. See Menéndez Pidal, *Romancero Hispánico*, I, 241 and *n.* 95; id., *Romancero tradicional* (Madrid, 1963), II, 125–126.

BALLADS FROM BOSNIA IN THE PRESENT
COLLECTION AND IN OTHER PUBLISHED SOURCES

Title (MP number)	A	B	C	Other Sources
1. *Melisenda* (28)			1	Levy 12
2. *Idólatra* (40)				*Rom. can.* 30
3. *Hero y Leandro* (41)		3	2	
4. *Virgilios* (46)	1	1	3	Pulido 296
5. *Reina y cautiva* (48)		11	4	
6. *Don Bueso* (49)			5	*Rom. Hisp.*, II, 338
7. *Conde Olinos* (55)		2	6	
8. ¿ *Por qué no cantáis?* (57)				*Spomenica* 323 *Rom. Hisp.*, II, 338
9. *Vuelta* (i) (58)		6	7	Jungić 2, Wiener 8 Levy 7
10. *Novia abandonada* (67)			8	
11. *Sueño profético* (68)		19		
12. *Parto en l. tierras* (68)		10	9	Jungić 1
13. *Malc. del pastor* (72)			10	Wiener 9
14. *Mujer engañada* (74)			11	
15. *Adúltera* (ó) (78)			12	
16. *Adúltera* (á-a) (80)			13A-B	Levy 85
17. *Landarico* (82)		8		Wiener 11, Levy 14 *Rom. Hisp.*, II, 217
18. *Bernal Francés* (83)		9		*Rom. Hisp.*, I, 362
19. *Rico Franco* (85)	2	15		
20. *Raptor pordiosero* (92)			14	
21. *Silvana* (98)	3	16		
22. *Delgadina* (99)			15	
23. *Tiempo es* (103)				Baruch, "J.-Esp.," p. 139
24. *Infanta deshonrada* (106)	4			

Title (MP number)	A	B	C	Other Sources
25. *Princesa y segador* (108)		5	15	
26. *Caballero burlado* (114)				Wiener 7
27. *Pendón* (120)			16	Levy 67, *Rom. Hisp.*, II, 180, 338
28. *Doncella guerrera* (121)		14	17	
29. *Hijo maldecido* (124)		12	18	*Rom. trad.*, III, 106 ff.
30. *Encuentro del padre* (125)	5	13	19	Wiener 12
31. *Escogiendo novia* (130)				Pulido 79
32. *Choza del desesp.* (140)		4	I	Levy 12
33. *Chuflete* (142)		17	20	
34. *Vuelta* (á-a)		7		
35. *Celinos*			16	Levy 67
36. *Conversa*			21	
37. *Fuerza de la sangre*				Wiener 7 D. Catalán 451
38. *Dama y pastor*				*Rom. Hisp.*, I, 341
39. *Canción del huérfano*				D. Catalán 458
40. *Bonetero*				*Por campos* 283

BIBLIOGRAPHY

JUDEO-SPANISH BALLADS:

Adatto (Schlesinger), E., "A Study of the Linguistic Characteristics of the Seattle Sefardí Folklore," Master's thesis, University of Washington, Seattle, 1935.

Algazi, L., *Chants séphardis*, London, 1958.

Armistead, S. G., and J. H. Silverman, "Dos romances fronterizos en la tradición sefardí oriental," *NRFH*, XIII (1959), 88–98.

——— "Hispanic Balladry among the Sephardic Jews of the West Coast," *WF*, XIX (1960), 229–244.

——— "Algo más para la bibliografía de Yacob Abraham Yoná," *NRFH*, XVII (1963–1964), 315–337.

——— "Christian Elements and De-Christianization in the Sephardic *Romancero*," in *Collected Studies in Honour of Américo Castro's Eightieth Year* (Oxford, England, 1965), pp. 21–38.

——— "A New Collection of Judeo-Spanish Ballads," *JFI*, III (1966), 133–153.

Attias, M., *Romancero sefaradí*, 1st ed., Jerusalem, 1956; 2d ed., Jerusalem, 1961.

Baruch, Kalmi, "Španske romanse bosanskih Jevreja," *Godišnjak izdaju La Benevolencia i Potpora* (Sarajevo-Belgrade, 1933), pp. 272–288.

Bassan (Warner), S., "Judeo-Spanish Folk Poetry," Master's thesis, Columbia University, New York, 1947.

Bénichou, P., *Romancero judeo-español de Marruecos*, Madrid, 1968. We cite page numbers (in parentheses) from this edition. Ballad numbers following the author's name refer to the earlier edition: "Romances judeo-españoles de Marruecos," *RFH*, VI (1944), 36–76, 105–138, 255–279, 313–381.

Catalán, Diego, *Por campos del Romancero: Estudios sobre la tradición oral moderna*, Madrid, 1970.

Danon, A., "Recueil de romances judéo-espagnoles chantées en Turquie," *REJ*, XXXII (1896), 102–123, 263–275; XXXIII (1896), 122–139, 255–268.

DRH = Armistead, S. G., and J. H. Silverman, *Diez romances hispánicos en un manuscrito sefardí de la Isla de Rodas*, Pisa, 1962.

Elnecavé, D., "Folklore de los sefardíes de Turquía," reprinted from *Sef*, XXIII (1963). References allude to the ballad numbers in Section III.

Estrugo, J. M., *Los sefardíes*, Havana, 1958.

González-Llubera, Ig., "Three Jewish Spanish Ballads in MS. *British Museum Add*. 26967," *MAe*, VII (1938), 15–28.

Idelsohn, A. Z., *Hebräisch-Orientalischer Melodienschatz. Band IV: Gesänge der orientalischen Sefardim*, Jerusalem-Berlin-Vienna, 1923.

Jungić, B., "Tri sefardske romanse," *Godišnjak izdaju La Benevolencia i Potpora* (Sarajevo-Belgrade, 1933), pp. 289–292.

Kamhi, S., "Jezik, pjesme i poslovice bosansko-hercegovačkih Sefarada," in *Spomenica*, pp. 105–121.

Katz, I. J., "Judeo-Spanish Traditional Ballads from Jerusalem," 2 vols., Doctoral thesis, University of California, Los Angeles, 1967 (to be published by The Institute of Mediaeval Music, Brooklyn, N.Y., 1971).

Larrea Palacín, A. de, *Romances de Tetuán*, 2 vols., Madrid, 1952.

Levy, I., *Chants judéo-espagnols*, London, [1959].

Levy [Lida], D., "El sefardí esmirniano de Nueva York," Doctoral thesis, Universidad Nacional Autónoma de México, 1952.

Molho, M., *Literatura sefardita de Oriente*, Madrid-Barcelona, 1960.

MP = Menéndez Pidal, R., "Catálogo del romancero judío-español," *CE*, I (1906), 1045–1077; V (1907), 161–199.

NSR = Armistead, S. G., and J. H. Silverman, "A New Sephardic *Romancero* from Salonika," *RPh*, XVI (1962–1963), 59–82.

Ortega, M. L., *Los hebreos en Marruecos*, 4th ed., Madrid, 1934.

Pulido Fernández, A., *Intereses nacionales: Españoles sin patria y la raza sefardí*, Madrid, 1905.

SICh = Armistead, S. G., and J. H. Silverman, "Judeo-Spanish Ballads in a MS by Salomon Israel Cherezli," *Studies in Honor of M. J. Benardete* (New York, 1965), pp. 367–387.

Spomenica = *Spomenica: 400 godina od dolaska Jevreja u Bosnu i Hercegovinu (1566–1966)*, Sarajevo, 1966.

Wiener, L., "Songs of the Spanish Jews in the Balkan Peninsula," *MPh*, I (1903–1904), 205–216, 259–274.

Yoná = Armistead, S. G., and J. H. Silverman, *The Judeo-Spanish Ballad Chapbooks of Yacob Abraham Yoná*, Berkeley–Los Angeles, 1970.

PENINSULAR AND HISPANO-AMERICAN BALLADS:

AFC = Amades, J., *Folklore de Catalunya: Cançoner (Cançons–Refranys–Endevinalles)*, Barcelona, 1951.

Aguiló y Fuster, M., *Romancer popular de la terra catalana: Cançons feudals cavalleresques*, Barcelona, 1893.

ART = Alonso Cortés, N., "Romances tradicionales," *RHi*, L (1920), 198–268.

ASW = Menéndez Pelayo, M., "Apéndices y suplemento a la *Primavera y flor de romances* de Wolf y Hoffmann," *Antología de poetas líricos castellanos*, IX, "Ed. Nac.," XXV, Santander, 1945.

Avenç, I = *40 cançons populars catalanes: Primera serie*, 2d ed., Barcelona: Biblioteca Popular de "L'Avenç," 1909.

Braga, Th., *Romanceiro geral português*, 2d ed., 3 vols., Lisbon, 1906, 1907, 1909.

Briz, F. P., *Cansons de la terra: Cants populars catalans*, 5 vols., I, Barcelona, 1866; II, Barcelona, 1867; III, Barcelona, 1871; IV, Barcelona-Paris, 1874; V, Barcelona-Paris, 1877.

Bulbena y Tosell, A. (alias Ali-Ben-Noab-Tun), *Romancer popular català*, Barcelona, 1900.

Capmany, A., *Cançoner popular*, 3 series, Barcelona, 1901–1903, 1904–1907, [1907]–1913.

Carré Alvarellos, L., *Romanceiro popular galego de tradizón oral*, Oporto, 1959.

Catalán, D., "A caza de romances raros en la tradición portuguesa," *Actas do III Colóquio Internacional de Estudos Luso-Brasileiros*, I (Lisbon, 1959), 445–477.

Cejador y Frauca, J., *La verdadera poesía castellana: Floresta de la antigua lírica popular*, 9 vols. + Index, I–II, Madrid, 1921; III, 1922; IV, 1923; V, 1924; VI–IX and Index, 1930.

CPE = Gil, B., *Cancionero popular de Extremadura*, 2 vols., I, 2d ed., Badajoz, 1961; II, Badajoz, 1956.

Fernández-Núñez, M. F., *Folk-lore leonés*, Madrid, 1931.

Frenk Alatorre, M., *La lírica popular en los siglos de oro*, Mexico City, 1946.

———— "Supervivencias de la antigua lírica popular," *Homenaje ofrecido a Dámaso Alonso*, I (Madrid, 1960), 51–78.

———— *Lírica hispánica de tipo popular (Edad Media y Renacimiento)*, Mexico City, 1966.

Furtado de Mendonça, M. A., "Romances populares da Beira-Baixa," *RL*, XIV (1911), 1–35.

Llorens de Serra, S., *Folklore de La Maresma, I: El Cançoner de Pineda (238 cançons populars amb 210 tonades)*, Barcelona, 1931.

Menéndez Pidal, R., "Poesía popular y poesía tradicional en la literatura española," in *Los romances de América y otros estudios*, 5th ed. (Buenos Aires–Mexico City: "Austral," 1948), pp. 52–91.

———— *Romancero Hispánico (hispano-portugués, americano y sefardí)*, 2 vols., Madrid, 1953.

———— *Romancero tradicional de las lenguas hispánicas (español-portugués-catalán-sefardí)*, 3 vols., Madrid, 1957, 1963, 1969.

Milá y Fontanals, M., *Romancerillo catalán: Canciones tradicionales*, 2d ed., Barcelona, 1882.

Morales, M., and M. J. López de Vergara, *Romancerillo canario: Catálogo-manual de recolección*, La Laguna, n. d. Introduction ("La recolección romancística en Canarias") by Diego Catalán (pp. [3–35]) dated May, 1955.

Nunes, J. J., "Subsídios para o Romanceiro português (Tradição popular do Algarve)," *RL*, VI (1900–1901), 151–188.

OCPC = *Obra del Cançoner popular de Catalunya: Materials*, 3 vols., I, fasc. 1, Barcelona, 1926; I, fasc. 2, II, Barcelona, 1928; III, Barcelona, 1929.

Pereira da Costa, F. A., "Folklore pernambucano: Romanceiro," *RIHGB*, LXX (1907), 295–641.

Primavera = Wolf, F. J., and C. Hofmann, *Primavera y flor de romances*, 2d ed., M. Menéndez Pelayo, *Antología de poetas líricos castellanos*, VIII, "Ed. Nac.," XXIV, Santander, 1945.

Reis Dâmaso, A., "Tradições populares (Colecção do Algarve): Romances," *Enciclopédia Republicana* (Lisbon, 1882), pp. 154–156, 171–173, 184; continued with the variant title: "Tradições populares do Algarve: Romances," pp. 201–204, 215–216, 232–237.

Rodríguez Marín, F., *Cantos populares españoles*, 5 vols., Madrid, n.d.

Romero, S., *Cantos populares do Brasil*, 2 vols., Rio de Janeiro, 1954.

RPC = Alonso Cortés, N., *Romances populares de Castilla*, Valladolid, 1906.

RPM = Cossío, J. M. de, and T. Maza Solano, *Romancero popular de La Montaña: Colección de romances tradicionales*, 2 vols., Santander, 1933–1934.

RTCN = *Romances tradicionales y canciones narrativas existentes en el Folklore español (incipit y temas)*, Barcelona: Instituto Español de Musicología, 1945.

Sampedro y Folgar, C., and J. Filgueira Valverde, *Cancionero musical de Galicia*, 2 vols., Madrid, 1942.

Tavares, J. A., "Romanceiro trasmontano," *RL*, VIII (1903–1905), 71–80; IX (1906), 277–323.

Vasconcellos, "Bibl. do Povo" = Leite de Vasconcellos, J., *Romanceiro português*, Lisbon: "Biblioteca do Povo e das Escolas," 1886.

VRP = Leite de Vasconcellos, J., *Romanceiro português*, 2 vols., Coimbra, 1958–1960.

EUROPEAN BALLADS:

Arbaud, D., *Chants populaires de la Provence*, 2 vols., Aix, 1862–1864.

Barbeau, M., *Le rossignol y chante*, Ottawa, 1962.

Barbeau, M., and E. Sapir, *Folk Songs of French Canada*, New Haven, 1925.

Child, F. J., *The English and Scottish Popular Ballads*, 5 vols., New York, 1965.

Davenson, H., *Le livre des chansons*, 3rd ed., Neuchâtel-Paris, 1955.

Decombe, L., *Chansons populaires recueillies dans le département d'Ille-et-Vilaine*, Rennes, 1884.

DgF = Grundtvig, S., with A. Olrik, H. Grüner Nielsen, and E. Abrahamsen, *Danmarks gamle Folkeviser*, 10 vols., Copenhagen, 1966–1967.

DVM = Meier, J., with E. Seemann, W. Wiora, H. Siuts, et al., *Deutsche Volkslieder mit ihren Melodien: Deutsche Volkslieder: Balladen*, 5 vols., I, Berlin-Leipzig, 1935; II, Berlin, 1939; III, 1954; IV, 1959; V, Freiburg-Breisgau, 1967.

Gagnon, E., *Chansons populaires du Canada*, Montreal, 1925.

Leader, N. A. M., *Hungarian Classical Ballads and Their Folklore*, Cambridge, England, 1967.

Mlotek, E. G., "International Motifs in the Yiddish Ballad," in *Studies in Jewish Languages, Literature, and Society: For Max Weinreich on His Seventieth Birthday* (The Hague, 1964), pp. 209–228.

Nigra, C., *Canti popolari del Piemonte*, Turin, 1957.

Poueigh, J., *Chansons populaires des Pyrénées françaises (Traditions-moeurs-usages)*, I, Paris-Auch, 1926.

Rolland, E., *Recueil de chansons populaires*, 6 vols., I, Paris, 1883; II, 1886; III–V, 1887; VI, 1890; reprinted in 3 vols., Paris, 1967.

Schirmunski, V., *Vergleichende Epenforschung*, I, Berlin, 1961.

Strausz, A., *Bulgarische Volksdichtungen*, Vienna-Leipzig, 1895.

INDICES

TITLES OF BALLADS AND EPICS

References are to pages (p. 1), to ballad numbers (A1), or to the section entitled "English Abstracts and Notes" (A1*n*).

FIRST VERSES

¿ De qué lloras, Blanca Niña ?   B12.
Día di vjernis di manjanika   C21.

¡ Džam, džam, farfulí findžán!   C11.

Eja era una mužer pompoza   C16.
El buen rej si hue a la gera   C12.
El buen rej tiene una iža   C15.
El buen rey tenía una hija   B15.
El rey tiene una hija   B5.
En la mar hay una torre   pp. 62, 100–101.
Estávase la condesa   p. 6.

Hija mía, mi querida   B2.

Irme quero, la mi madre   B4.
'I 'una 'iža tyene 'el rey   A2.
Iža mía, mi kerida   C6.

Jirme kero, la me madre   C1.

Kaminando por altas mares   A5.
Kaminí por altas tores   C19.
Ken kere tomar konsežo   C16.
Ken madre no tiene   C9.

Labrando estaba la reina   B9.
La reina de Francia   B19.
La reina Xarifa mora   p. 51.
¿ Lo ke joráš, Blanka Njinja ?   C18.

Mal grado se iba Don Vergile   B1.
Mañanita era, mañana   p. 40.
Mariquita me llaman   B18n.
Mi madre era di Brusa   C10.
Mi madre era di Francia   C10 (variant).
Morena me llaman   B18.
Morenica a mí me llaman   B18n.
Morenico sos, querido   B20.
Morenita resalada   B18n.
Moricos, los mis moricos   B11.
Morikos, los mis morikos   C4.
Muéro-me mi alma   p. 39, n. 7.
Měrômê ᵉal mah   p. 39, n. 7.

¡ Noćes, noćes, buenas noćes …!   C1.

Parida 'está la 'infanta   A4.
Pasear se ía Silvana   B16.
[Paseáva]se Silbana   A3.
Pasióse Doverdjeli   C3.
Prigoneros van i vjenen   C17.

Quien madre no tiene   p. 59.

Salir kere el mez de mart   C20.
Salir quere el mes de marzo   B17.
Salteñito me dicen   B18n.
Siete anjos andava   C14.

Tiempo es el caballero   p. 6.
Tra'isyyones al Don Virğile   A1.
Tres hermanicas (ellas) eran   B3.
Trez ermanikas eran   C2.

Una tarde de las tardes   C8.

MOTIFS

From S. Thompson, *Motif-Index of Folk-Literature*, 2d ed., 6 vols., Bloomington, 1955–1958. References are to the section, "English Abstracts and Notes."

B. ANIMALS

| B81. | *Mermaid*: B2. |
| B211.2.2. | *Speaking lion*: A5. |

D. MAGIC

D233.	*Transformation: man to shell*: B2.
D237.	*Transformation: man to coral*: B2.
D1039.2.	*Magic salt*: B10.
D1051.	*Magic cloth*: C16.
D1223.1.	*Magic flute*: B17.
D1224.	*Magic pipe (musical)*: B17.
D1224.1.	*Magic flageolet*: B17.
D1225.	*Magic whistle*: B17.
D1275.1.	*Magic music*: B17.
D1275.2.	*Magic melody*: B17.
D1426.1.	*Magic flute compels woman to come to man*: B17.
D1501.2.	*Charms make childbirth easy*: B10; cf. B17.
D1523.2.6.	*Boat guided by magic songs*: B17.
D1782.	*Sympathetic magic*: B10.
D1812.3.3.	*Future revealed in dream*: B19.
D1812.3.3.5.	*Prophetic dream allegorical*: B19.
D1812.3.3.9.	*Future husband revealed in dream*: B19.
D2088.	*Locks opened by magic*: B17.

E. THE DEAD

E613.	*Reincarnation as bird*: B2.
E613.3.	*Reincarnation as hawk*: B2.
E613.6.	*Reincarnation as dove*: B2.

F. MARVELS

F811.	*Extraordinary tree*: B6.
F811.1.1.	*Golden tree*: B6.
F811.1.7.	*Tree with silver trunk, gold branches, etc.*: B6.
F821.1.1.	*Golden clothes*: C5.
F843.1.	*Rope made of person's hair*: B3, B6.
F848.1.	*Girl's long hair as ladder into tower*: B3, B6.
F1041.1.2.2.4.	*Death from hearing of son's death*: B12.

H. TESTS

H12.	*Recognition by song (music)*: B11.
H51.1.	*Recognition by birthmark*: B6.
H110.	*Identification by cloth*: C16.
H1385.5.	*Quest for vanished lover*: C8.
H1385.7.	*Quest for lost father*: A5.
H1385.8.	*Quest for lost brother*: A5.
H1556.	*Tests of fidelity*: B6, B7, C10.
H1556.2.	*Test of fidelity through submitting hero* (hero's wife) *to temptations*: B6, C10.
H1578.	*Test of sex: to discover person masking as of other sex*: B14.
H1578.1.	*Test of sex of girl masking as man*: B14.

J. THE WISE AND THE FOOLISH

J445.2.	*Foolish marriage of old man and young girl*: C16.
J642.	*Foolishness of surrendering weapons*: A2.

K. DECEPTIONS

K631.	*Captor induced to disarm himself*: A2.
K818.	*Victim persuaded to disarm. Killed*: A2.
K818.1.	*Man killed with sword, which he himself is tricked into passing to captured enemy*: A2.
K910.	*Murder by strategy*: A2.
K955.	*Murder by burning*: A2.
K1212.	*Lover left standing in snow while his mistress is with another*: C13.
K1223.2.1.	*Chaste woman sends man's own wife as substitute (without his knowledge)*: A3.
K1227.1.	*Lover put off till girl bathes and dresses*: A3.
K1317.5.	*Woman substitutes for her daughter in the dark*: A3.
K1349.2.	*(Attempted seduction) by pretending to have news of absent lover* (husband): B6.
K1500.	*Deception connected with adultery*: B8, C11, C12, C13.
K1550.	*Husband outwits adulteress and paramour*: C13.
K1550.1.	*Husband discovers wife's adultery*: B8, B9, C12, C13.
K1817.1.	*Disguise as beggar*: C14.
K1817.2.	*Disguise as palmer (pilgrim)*: B9, C14.

K1837.	*Disguise of woman in man's clothes*: B14.
K1837.6.	*Disguise of woman as a soldier*: B14.
K1847.	*Deception by substitution of children*: B11.
K1860.	*Deception by feigned death*: B12.

L. REVERSAL OF FORTUNE

L113.1.0.1.	*Heroine endures hardships with menial husband*: C16.
L410.5.	*King overthrown and made servant*: A2.

M. ORDAINING THE FUTURE

M411.1.	*Curse by parent*: B12.

N. CHANCE AND FATE

N2.6.2.	*Daughter as wager*: A2.
N344.	*Father* (mother) *kills self* (attempts to kill self) *believing that son* (daughter) *is dead*: B10, B12.
N711.1.	*King* (prince) *finds maiden in woods* (tree) . . . : B6.
N715.1.	*Hero finds maiden at fountain* (well, river): C5.

P. SOCIETY

P313.1.	*Babies exchanged*: B11.
P678.1.	*Tearing garments as sign of grief*: A5.

Q. REWARDS AND PUNISHMENTS

Q256.	*Punishment for clandestine lover of princess*: A4.
Q411.	*Death as punishment*: A4, A5.
Q411.0.1.	*Husband kills . . . adulteress*: B8, B9, C12.
Q421.0.2.	*Beheading as punishment for adultery*: B8, B9.
Q433.	*Punishment: imprisonment*: C15.
Q433.5.	*Imprisonment for* (attempted) *seduction*: A1.
Q465.3.	*Punishment: pushing into well*: A5.
Q501.7.1.	*Salt food without drink as punishment*: C15.

R. CAPTIVES AND FUGITIVES

R10.1.	*Princess* (maiden) *abducted*: A2, B11, C5, C14.
R41.	*Captivity in tower* (castle, prison): C15.
R41.2.	*Captivity in tower*: B3, B5, Jungić 3.

S. UNNATURAL CRUELTY

S51.1.	*Cruel mother-in-law plans death of daughter-in-law*: B10.
S112.	*Burning to death*: A2.
S146.1.	*Abandonment in well*: A5.
S161.	*Mutilation: cutting off hands* (arms): A2, C12.
S180.	*Torturing*: A2, C12.

T. SEX

T35.1.	*Fountain (well) as lovers' rendezvous*: C10.
T50.1.2.	*Girl carefully guarded by father*: B3, B5.
T55.	*Girl as wooer: Forthputting woman*: B5.
T55.1.	*Princess declares her love for lowly hero*: B5.
T61.2.	*Parting lovers pledge not to marry for seven years*: B12.
T80.	*Tragic love*: B2, B4.
T83.	*Hero and Leander*: B3.
T91.	*Unequals in love*: B5, C14.
T91.6.4.	*Princess falls in love with lowly boy*: B5.
T93.2.	*Disappointed lover turns hermit*: B4.
T93.3.	*Disappointed lover kills self*: B4.
T121.	*Unequal marriage*: C16.
T230.	*Faithlessness in marriage*: B8, B9, C11, C12, C13.
T257.1.	*Woman jealous of a fair maid in her house*: C5.
T381.	*Imprisoned virgin to prevent knowledge of men: Usually kept in a tower*: B5.
T410.	*Incest*: A3, C15.
T411.	*Father-daughter incest*: A3, C15.
T411.1.	*Lecherous father. Unnatural father wants to marry his daughter*: A3, C15.
T481.	*Adultery*: B8, B9, C11, C12, C13.
T574.	*Long pregnancy. Delayed by an enemy who bewitches the mother*: B10.
T582.3.	*Knots to be untied at childbirth*: B10.
T640.	*Illegitimate children*: A4.

V. RELIGION

V115.	*Church bells*: B10.
V331.5.	*Conversion to Christianity* (Islam) *through love*: C21.

W. TRAITS OF CHARACTER

W131.1.	*Profligate wastes entire fortune...*: C16.

Z. MISCELLANEOUS GROUPS OF MOTIFS

Z71.5.	*Formulistic number: seven*: C11, C14.

GLOSSARY

With the exception of Turkisms and Hebraisms, all of which are included, we list only those Judeo-Spanish forms which are in some way lexically, semantically, or phonologically remarkable and which are not to be found in C. Crews, *Recherches sur le judéo-espagnol dans les pays balkaniques* (Paris, 1935). Turkish references follow the *New Redhouse Turkish-English Dictionary* (Istanbul, 1968); Serbo-Croatian Turkisms are cited according to A. Knežević, *Die Turzismen in der Sprache der Kroaten und Serben* (Meisenheim am Glan, 1962) and/or B. Klaić, *Veliki rječnik stranih riječi*, 4th ed. (Zagreb, 1966). The following works are also referred to:

Baruch, K., "El judeo-español de Bosnia," *RFE*, XVII (1930), 113–151.

DCELC = J. Corominas, *Diccionario crítico etimológico de la lengua castellana*, 4 vols., Madrid, 1954.

Gaspar Remiro, M., "Vocablos y frases del judeo-español (Segunda serie)," *BAE*, III (1916), 67–74, 186–196, 498–509; IV (1917), 107–121, 327–335, 459–468, 631–642; V (1918), 350–364.

Luria, M. A., *A Study of the Monastir Dialect of Judeo-Spanish Based on Oral Material Collected in Monastir, Yugo-slavia*, New York, 1930.

Miklosich, F. "Die Türkischen Elemente in den südost- und osteuropäischen Sprachen," *Denkschriften der Kaiserlichen Akademie der Wissenschaften: Philosophisch-Historische Classe*, 34 (1884), 239–338; 35 (1885), 105–192.

Saporta y Beja, E., *Refranero sefardí*, Madrid-Barcelona, 1957.

Simon, W., "Charakteristik des judenspanischen Dialekts von Saloniki," *ZRPh*, XL (1920), 655–689.

Subak, J., "Zum Judenspanischen," *ZRPh*, XXX (1906), 129–185.

Wagner, M. L., "Los dialectos judeoespañoles de Karaferia, Kastoria y Brusa," *Homenaje a Menéndez Pidal*, II (1924), 193–203.

―――― *Caracteres generales del judeo-español de Oriente*, Madrid, 1930.

Yahuda, A. S., "Contribución al estudio del judeo-español," *RFE*, II (1915), 339–370.

aboracar 'to pierce' B16.4; *aborracar* B7.9; see Luria 169.

abramar 'to roar' C19.4.

acapitar 'to happen' B14.21 (It. *capitare*); Baruch, pp. 122, 149, *n*. 2.

afarar 'to sieze' C13A.15, 17, C13B.7. Concerning this and other forms in which -*er*- > -*ar*- see Baruch, pp. 124, 125, 132; Subak, p. 141; Wagner, "Karaferia," p. 200; id., *Caracteres*, p. 18.

afrito 'sad, afflicted' C9.39, 41. The word occurs in an *endecha* published by M. Attias, "θišᶜāh bĕ-Āb," *Salonique: Ville-Mère en Israël* (Jerusalem-Tel-Aviv, 1967), p. 171a (O. Sp. *aflicto, aflito*). See *DCELC*, s. v. *afligir*. *Afreir* figures in Medieval J.-Sp. Bible translations. See Gaspar Remiro, *BAE*, III, 190–191, who also notes the use of *aflito* in the Ferrara Bible. Molho lists *afrito* as 'deseoso, hambriento' (*Literatura sefardita*, p. 377).

aǧiprés 'cypress' A2.14 (Meaningless in this context).

ajde 'Hurry up!, Get along!' C21.7, 11 (T. *haydi*; SC. *hàjde, hâjde, àjde, ăjde*); see Crews 599; Luria 127, 176; also *DCELC*, I, 278a.

alda 'skirt' A4.6, 8 (here, some article of men's clothing).

almoza 'alms' C14.4, 6, 8, 10; Cf. O. Sp. *almosna*; see *DCELC*, s. v. *limosna*.

amán 'have mercy!' A3 (refrain) (T. *aman*; SC. *àmān*); see Crews 837, Luria 176; Miklosich, s.v.

Anadol 'Anatolia' C12.1, 16, 24, C17.1 (T. *Anadolu*; Serb. *Ànadōl*; cf. Miklosich, p. 247).

apodzar 'to alight, come to rest' C6.12, 14; Baruch, p. 134.

aprevar 'to test' C10.6, C17.22; see Crews 191 (*prevar*), Luria 37 (*aprivar*, *privar*); see also *preva*.

april 'April' C20.1 (*SC àprīl*); cf. Wagner, "Karaferia," p. 197.

armadas 'arms, armor' C12.22, 23.

baltá 'hatchet, axe' C13A.22, C13B.8 (T. *balta*; SC. *bâlta, bàlta*); see Luria 176; Miklosich, s.v.

bel 'waist' B15.22 (T. *bel*); see Crews 693.

ben 'mole' C7.22 (T. *ben*; SC. *bên, bĕn*); see Miklosich, s.v.; Crews 1346 (*benk*).

benear 'to mount, ride' B8.10 (T. *bin*-; SC. *binj*- [in various derivatives]); see also *enbenejar*; Cf. Miklosich, s.v. *binék*.

bolisa 'lady' C7.6, 7, 11, 15, 19, 21, 23 (T. *boliçe* 'Jewish girl'); Cf. NSR, p. 79.

buba: nonsense word used in rocking a child to sleep B11.13, 25, C4.21.

cadir: See **kadir**.

chuflete 'flute, whistle' B17.5,7,13; *čuflet* C20.4, 11; see Crews, s.v. *čuflet*; Yoná 13, *n*. 7, 27, *nn*. 7–9.

debló n 'doubloon' C18.7.

doler: *güelen* B9.7. Is this simply a substitution of *g*- for *d*-, or has apheresis operated on the typically J.-Sp. form *digüelen* ('duelen')?

[džak]et 'jacket' C17.15. We suppose the existence of a J.-Sp. form based upon T. *caket* or perhaps directly from F. *jaquette*. Luria (p. 224a) records *ğaquete*, which he derives from It. *giacchetta*. Another possibility would be *žaket*, based on SC. *žàkēt*.

džam 'glass, window' C11.1, 2 (T. *cam*; SC. *džȁm*); see Crews 619; Miklosich, s.v.

enbenejar 'ride' C3.20 (T. *bin*-; SC. *binj*-); see also *benear*.

enlugo 'immediately' C9.25 (Port. *logo*). Luria records *inluegu* and *inilugu*; Baruch lists *lugu*, *inlugu*, *ilugu* (pp. 124, *n*. 4, 147, *n*. 7).

enstonses 'then' C5.38.

entarar 'to bury' C21.12.

escribanica 'fan' or 'writing pen' (?) B9.2.

eskontrar 'to find, to meet' C8.2, 7; see Luria 2 (*iscontru* 'encuentro').

eskoza 'betrothed' C17.22; see Gaspar Remiro, *BAE*, IV, 631–632; DCELC s. v. *escosa*. Here the form is certainly confused with *esposa*.

farfulí 'chinaware, of porcelain' C11.1 (T. *faǧfurî*); see Miklosich, s.v. *fagfur*; the variant *farfurî* exists in T. and various Balkan languages.

feredžé 'woman's overcoat' C21.2 (var.) (T. *ferace*, *fereci* 'dustcoat formerly worn by Turkish women when they went out'; SC. *fèredža* 'Oberkleid m. langen Ärmeln, Kopfschleier').

férida 'fair' C20.12.

findžán 'cup'. C11.1 (T. *fincan*; SC. *fìndžān*, *fìldžān*); see Luria, s.v. *filǧán*; Miklosich, s.v. *fildžan*.

finel 'torch' B15.14. (T. *fener* 'lantern'; SC. *fènjer* 'id.'); see Miklosich, s.v. *fénér*; also *RPh*, XXII (1968–1969), 240–241.

ganado 'profit' C13A.5; see Yoná 10, *n.* 12.

ginquilí meaning? B6.15.

gizandero 'cook' A2.8; *guisandera* B15.11.

güelen: See **doler.**

gustižo 'capricious desire' A4.9.

ǧanim 'my soul' A2 (refrain) (T. *canım*; SC. *džănum*); see Crews 1180 (*ǧane,* *-u*); Miklosich, s.v. *džan.*

haham 'rabbi' C11.25, C21.3 (H. *ḥākām*); see Crews 311; Luria 175; Simon, p. 687.

jarif 'graceful, delicate' B6.3, B15.1 (T. *zarif*?). Cf. Miklosich, s.v. *zarif.* Sp. *jarifo,* O. Sp. *xarifo,* should equal J.-Sp. **šarifo.*

jelada 'frost, ice' C13A.9; see Luria 165 (*yilade*).

jelado 'freezing' C5.23, 25.

ješivá 'school, assembly' C21.11 (H. *yĕšîbāh*).

kadir 'able, capable' C8.4, 5; *cadir* B9.7 (T. *kadir*; SC. *kádar, káder*); see Baruch, p. 143, *n.* 7; Luria 176; Miklosich, s.v.

karsel 'prison' C3.5, 13, 14, 16.

karseljo 'prison' C3.6, 7, 15.

kermezí 'red' B9.17 (T. *kırmızı*; SC. *krmzi*); Cf. Miklosich, p. 332. For reasons against a direct relationship with Sp. *carmesí,* see *DCELC,* I, 691a.

klavidón 'gold wire wound on silk, gilt copper wire or thread' C16.12, 14, 17 (T. *kılaptan*; SC. *klobòdan*). The J.-Sp. form is based upon dialectal T. *klabudan*; see Crews 760, 967; Miklosich, s.v. *kẹlabdan.*

kompanjo 'companion' C5. 26; cf. O. Sp. *compaño*; see *DCELC,* s.v. *compañero.*

konak 'mansion, palace' B2.12, 14, C6.14 (T. *konak*; SC. *kònak*); see Crews 769; Miklosich, s.v. *konmak*; Simon, p. 688.

kondžá 'rose' B20.2 (T. *konca*); see Crews 1187; Luria 176 (*cunǧéru*).

konte 'count' C9.5, 7, 9, 11, C14.17, 19 (It. *conte*?).

kontor 'coat'? C12.5–7 (T. *kontoş*); see Miklosich, s.v. *kontoš.*

kuandro 'when' C5.33, 37 (typogr. error?).

kulaj 'easy, easily' C9.34 (T. *kolay*; SC. *kòlāj*); see Baruch, p. 127; Crews 1104; Luria 176; Miklosich, s.v. *kolaj*; Simon, p. 688.

kunduria 'shoe, slipper' C12.18, 19 (T. *kundura*; SC. *kòndura*); see Crews 574, 1306; Miklosich, s.v. *kondura*.

lutyyo 'mourning' A1.8, 10. (O. Port. *loito*?); see *DCELC*, *s.v. luto*; Wagner, "Karaferia," p. 197 (*lúito*).

luzía 'beautiful, bright' C5.9. Accentuation is imposed by the rhyme; normally *luzio*.

mala 'enkonyí'a 'melancholy' A3.21; see Yoná, Glossary, s.v.

mandzija 'misfortune' C14.21; see Baruch, p. 134; Luria, p. 218; Wagner, *Caracteres*, p. 17.

maromero 'pilgrim' C14.3, 7, 18, 22, 23 (<*mal romero*).

mart 'March' C20.1 (SC. *mart*). Cf. Wagner, "Karaferia," p. 197.

maví 'blue' C7.22 (T. *mavi*; SC. *mávi*); see Crews 521; Miklosich, s.v.

minguno 'no one' B1.9 (typogr. error?).

minhá 'afternoon prayer' C8.1, 6 (H. *minḥāh*).

mívos 'mine' C1.17.

nana: nonsense word used in rocking a child to sleep B11.13, 25, C4.21; see Crews 1101; Luria 127 (*nani*).

ničozas 'fortunate' C9.17 (read *dičozas*).

novjedad 'period of engagement or betrothal' C1.7.

odá 'room, chamber' B2.1; *udá* C6.1 (T. *oda*; SC. *òda, òdaja*); see Crews 611; Luria 176; Miklosich, s.v.; Simon, p. 689.

pačá 'leg' C5.25 (T. *paça* 'lower part of the leg'); see Miklosich, s.v.; Crews 482; Luria 176; Wagner, *Caracteres*, p. 72, n. 5.

palpos 'gropings' C14.10; *palpones* C14.10.

paltó 'coat' B14.12 (T. *palto*; SC. *pàlto*). Crews (127) records *paltón*. The word is probably not directly from Fr., as Luria maintains (173).

pansensja 'patience' C1.16. If this is not simply an error, it may be related to the proverb "La pacencia es pan i cencia" (Saporta, p. 229; Subak, p. 178).

parder 'to lose' C13A.18.

pašá 'pasha' B2.12, C6.12, C21.1, 10, 18 (T. *paşa*; SC. *pȁša, pàša*); see Crews 1219; Luria 176; Miklosich, s.v.

preva 'test' C10.6; see Luria, p. 98 (*preve*); Wagner, *Caracteres*, p. 108, *n.* 6; see also *aprevar*.

saver: *supyendo* A3.22. On pres. parts. formed with pret. stems see C. Crews, *RPh*, IX (1955–1956), 236; Luria 100a; Simon, 681 (¶ 28); Subak, pp. 129, 138; Wagner, *Caracteres*, p. 104, *n.* 6.

sanergir: See *sonergir*.

sarar 'to close' C11.14.

siarda 'left' C7.22.

siklejar 'to worry, grieve' C21.15 (T. *sıklet* 'heaviness, uneasiness, depression'); see Crews 760, 902; Luria 176; Miklosich, p. 156.

sirma 'silver gilt thread' C12.7, 12 (T. *sırma*; SC. *sȑma*); see Luria 176; Miklosich, p. 157.

sonergir 'to cause [a musical instrument] to sound' B17.6, 8; *sanergir* C20.4,5 (L. *ērĭgĕre*? originally 'to bring to life, to revive'?). On O. Sp. forms, including *erger* (*Libro de Alex.*), see *DCELC*, s.v. *erguir*; Y. Malkiel, *RPh*, XXII (1968–1969), 505–508.

taraínas 'preparation of dried curds and flour; soup made of this preparation' B11.7; *tarajinas* C4.17 (T. *tarhana*; SC. *taràna*); see Miklosich, p. 170. The penultimate syllable intrudes because of the rhyme. Cf. *amargina* (for *amarga*) C11.13.

temblar 'to tune' (?) A3.3.

tener: *tuvjendo* C21.14.

tesuá 'repentance' C21.7 (H. *tĕšúbāh*).

turundjí 'lemon balm' (?) B9.9 (Sp. *toronjil* ?; although possibly reinforced by T. *turunc* 'Seville orange, bitter orange'; T. *turuncu* 'orange (color)'; SC. *turûnǵi, turùndži* 'Farbe wie die Apfelsine').

udá: See **odá.**

vezir 'vizier, minister' B2.14, C6.14 (T. *vezir*; SC. *vèzīr*); see Crews 628; Luria 176, Miklosich, s.v.; Simon, p. 687.

vringuensa 'shame' C2.3. Crews records *vrngwensa* (49). For other forms, see Baruch, p. 147; Simon, p. 686.

zehorá 'melancholy' C21.15 (H. *mārāh šĕḥôrāh*); see Crews 725, 1169; Luria 175; Yahuda, p. 369.

zenđefil 'ginger' C7.13; *zeđefil* C7.9 (T. *zencefil*; SC. *zenđefil*); see Miklosich, s.v. *zéndžéfil*.